Dept. of Health + Catihning
Professional Studies .

CW01080298

Practical Pointers
for Quality Assessment

Bill Cox and Amanda Ingleby

**KOGAN
PAGE**

To Max, *BC*.

Amanda would like to dedicate this book to Teresa, Stanley, Jacqueline and Anthony.

First published in 1997

Apart from any fair dealing for the purposes of research or private study, or criticism or review, as permitted under the Copyright, Designs and Patents Act 1988, this publication may only be reproduced, stored or transmitted, in any form or by any means, with the prior permission in writing of the publishers, or in the case of reprographic reproduction in accordance with the terms of licences issued by the Copyright Licensing Agency. Enquiries concerning reproduction outside those terms should be sent to the publishers at the undermentioned address:

Kogan Page Limited
120 Pentonville Road
London N1 9JN
and
22883 Quicksilver Drive
Stirling, VA 20166, USA

© Bill Cox and Amanda Ingleby, 1997

British Library Cataloguing in Publication Data

A CIP record for this book is available from the British Library.

ISBN 0 7494 2187 8 hardback
ISBN 0 7494 2188 6 paperback

Typeset by Northern Phototypesetting Co Ltd, Bolton
Printed and bound in Great Britain by Biddles Ltd, Guildford and King's Lynn

Contents

Preface

When we first mooted the idea for this book, some well known and highly respected writers on professional and educational development in higher education expressed reservations, because quality assessment changes so fast. That, coupled with the fact that quality assessment covers the whole range of provision which makes up the complete student learning experience, has presented a unique challenge.

The academic practitioner needs to catch up with the general educational implications of quality assessment, and if this means freezing the frames momentarily then so be it. We have therefore produced a book which takes a broad and generic view of quality assessment and its implications for educational providers, including lecturing staff, senior/programme tutors, heads of department, support services staff, staff development, technicians, administrators, quality co-ordinators and heads of institutions.

Some things may have changed by the time you read this, but we believe that most of the material is sufficiently durable and portable to withstand this. For each aspect of provision, we have distilled a key set of issues based upon the *aide-mémoires* used under the Welsh and Scottish further education systems as well as the English system, and based upon our own experiences of quality assessment.

One of the most bewildering features of quality assessment is the vast number of constituencies, organizations, and professional bodies involved and the rate at which they change. For example, some HEI practitioners still refer to 'HEQC audit' when they mean 'HEFCE assessment'. We have found that the only way to keep up with the changes is to contact the various bodies directly. We therefore provide, in an appendix, a list of the main players in quality assessment and related matters.

Recent developments

Aiming to be as up-to-date as possible we summarize here a few of the most recent developments that have arisen since writing the main body of the book, which we have been able to incorporate at the last minute.

Further developments to look out for include:

- QAAHE to report on their five-year strategy
- John Randall (chief executive of the agency) identifies one of the important roles of the agency as raising the esteem of teaching in universities and colleges
- Christopher Kenyon (the chair of the agency) highlights standards, openness and self-regulation as the key issues for the agency
- a consultation exercise between QAAHE and institutions on a new integrated process of quality assurance (which builds upon audit and assessment) to be in place by October 1998
- speculation that the six core aspects of the HEFCE system may be reduced by dropping the Learning Resources aspect
- revisions in the training for assessors
- continued consultation on a funding model for teaching post-Dearing, which undoubtedly will give consideration to the role of quality assessment outcomes
- 'products' for dissemination arising from the fund for the development of teaching and learning (FDTL) projects
- further council initiatives on teaching and learning stimulated by a study to be conducted by Graham Gibbs on behalf of HEFCE.

We hope this book will be a useful resource in contributing to the continuing development of the quality assessment methodology as part of the consultation to take place between the QAAHE and HEIs in the UK.

Bill Cox and Amanda Ingleby

Acknowledgements

We would like to thank everyone who provided support and comment in the preparation of this book. Sarah Marshall for her patience and ideas in helping us analyse nearly 200 quality assessment reports in the early days of quality assessment; the results of which provided a rich source of information and a good foundation for writing this book. Many thanks to those HEFCE staff who provided clarification when we reached exasperation during many heated debates (particularly over aims, objectives and learning outcomes etc). We would also like to thank Sam Riley and Jacqueline Tonks for diligent proof-reading, and also Mary Dunne, a former English teacher of one of the authors, who reminded us of the falling standards in written English; Val Tyas for word-processing the chapters, interpreting our writing and forcing us to make sensible decisions; Pat Lomax and Liz Roberts for editorial assistance; Vaneta d'Andrea and Melinda Drowley for sharing their experiences and anecdotes; Denis Ager, Mike Cardwell, Rudiger Görner, John Maiden, Trevor Oliver, Nigel Reeves, Brian Tighe, John White, Mike Wilson and Mike Wrenn for sharing their experiences of quality assessment and involving us in preparation, the visit and in follow up. Particular thanks go to quality assessors at Aston who have provided us with useful feedback in our support of departments in preparation for assessment, including David Miller, Bernard Gilmartin and Phil Barker.

Abbreviations

AAU	Academic Audit Unit
CAL	computer-aided learning
CATS	Credit Accumulation and Transfer Scheme
CDCO	curriculum design, content and organization
CHES	Centre for Higher Education Studies
CNAA	Council for National Academic Awards
COSHEP	Committee of Scottish Higher Education Principals
CPD	continuing professional development
CVCP	Committee of Vice-Chancellors and Principals
DENI	Department of Education for Northern Ireland
DfEE	Department for Education and Employment
DQA	Division of Quality Audit (HEQC)
FDTL	Fund for the Development of Teaching and Learning
FEDA	Further Education Development Agency
FEFC	Further Education Funding Council
GCSE	General Certificate of Secondary Education
GSP	Graduate Standards Programme
HEFCE	Higher Education Funding Council for England
HEFCW	Higher Education Funding Council for Wales
HEI	higher education institution
HEQC	Higher Education Quality Council
HESA	Higher Education Statistics Agency
HMI	Her Majesty's Inspectorate
IT	information technology
JPG	Joint Planning Group
LR	learning resources
NUS	National Union of Students
PCFC	Polytechnics and Colleges Funding Council
PSB	Professional and Statutory Body
QAAHE	Quality Assurance Agency for Higher Education
QAD	Quality Assessment Division (HEFCE)
QAE	quality assurance and enhancement
QAM	quality assessment manager
QSC	Quality Support Centre
RAE	Research Assessment Exercise
RBL	resource-based learning
SCONUL	Standing Conference of National and University Libraries
SEDA	Staff and Educational Development Association
SHEFC	Scottish Higher Education Funding Council
SPA	student progression and achievement
SSA	subject specialist assessor
SSG	student support and guidance
TLA	teaching, learning and assessment
TLTP	Teaching and Learning Technology Programme
UCISA	Universities and Colleges Information Systems Association
UCoSDA	Universities' and Colleges' Staff Development Agency
UFC	Universities Funding Council

Chapter 1

Introduction

About this book

Objectives

The changing nature of quality assessment has proved a challenge in writing this book. As we write, the new Quality Assurance Agency for Higher Education (QAAHE) is about to manage the merger of the two quality processes – audit and assessment. The name of the process will change, from 'assessment' to 'review', and 'assessors' will become 'reviewers', although the current procedures and terminology for quality assessment will remain in place until September 1998, and we have structured this book so that the reader can easily incorporate subsequent changes. Inevitably an enterprise that attempts to introduce a nationwide accountability structure in higher education will have teething troubles and will need to adapt quickly. The underlying principles must evolve, for example from selective to universal visiting, but it is clear that all aspects of educational provision will continue to be subject to assessment of one form or another. This demands fundamental shifts in the way staff in higher education institutions (HEIs) regard and conduct their profession, which is the prime interest of this book.

Since it is applicable to most UK provision, we focus mainly on the English quality assessment system, employed by the Higher Education Funding Council for England (HEFCE). We have also made reference to the Scottish and Welsh systems and further education where appropriate. No doubt the HEFCE quality assessment system will continue to evolve and improve. We hope that this book will make a contribution to this, while at the same time helping providers to improve their performance in quality assessment. We believe that the current methodology could be an effective developmental

1

tool for higher education provision. This requires academic staff, assessors and all other stakeholders in higher education to reflect critically on the methodology, its operation and aim for continual improvements. Thus, our objectives are to:

- inform providers and other stakeholders in higher education about the quality assessment process and changes in prospect;
- help providers prepare for quality assessment and optimize the outcome;
- evaluate the quality assessment process, encourage constructive criticism and suggest improvements;
- disseminate the outcomes of quality assessment;
- promote the developmental opportunities provided by quality assessment.

Terminology

Due to the scope and technicality of quality assessment, we have had some difficulty with the terminology used, on which there is not always agreement. We have used terms that we hope will map easily onto your local jargon but there is also a difficulty in referring to the type of institution – some points and issues are relevant only to a subset of institutions, or to a particular sector, which can be cumbersome to specify.

Finally, there is the question of acronyms. Unfortunately, this subject is full of them: funding councils (HEFCE, SHEFC, etc), subject and professional bodies (UCoSDA, SEDA, etc), various committees or working groups (CVCP, JPG, etc), HEFCE shorthand (CDCO, TLA, etc). We have tried to keep acronyms to a minimum but it is impossible to avoid them entirely these days. A list of acronyms used in this book is given on page viii.

Structure of the book

Following this introductory chapter on the development of the quality assessment process, Chapter 2 describes the HEFCE quality assessment methodology and suggestions for responding to it. The first and very important stage for the subject provider is the preparation of the self-assessment and this is the subject of Chapter 3. HEFCE assesses provision in terms of *six core aspects* and we devote Chapters 4–9 to detailed study of each. The *Assessors' Handbook* (HEFCE, 1996a) provides the HEFCE assessors with an *aide-mémoire* for analysing the self-assessment, gathering evidence on the visit and preparing the final quality assessment report. This comprises a number of questions and serves as a useful prompt for assessors *and* assessees. This is our starting point in identifying a set of key issues in each of the aspects and forms the basis for Chapters 4–9. Chapter 10 looks at the preparation for and conduct of the assessment visit. Finally, Chapter 11 takes a brief look at some of the developmental outcomes of quality assessment, criticisms of the methodology, and future developments envisaged. The complexity of higher education provision, and the interrelationship of the many issues involved in quality assessment mean that some repetition of ideas and material between chapters is inevitable. While wishing to keep this to a minimum, we have occasionally compromised to make some of the chapters self-contained.

When using this book it would be helpful, though not essential, to have the following funding council documentation to hand:

HEFCE Circular 39/94 *The Quality Assessment Method from April 1995*
HEFCE Circular 26/95 *Quality Assessment Between October 1996 and September 1998*
HEFCE *Assessors' Handbook October 1996 to September 1998*
HEFCE *Report(s) on Quality Assessment 1992–95 and 1995–96*

Apart from the *Assessors' Handbook* these are all free on the Web (http://www.niss.ac.uk/education/hefce/).

HEFCE has a number of subject contacts for the subjects currently under assessment, to which enquiries may be made on all quality assessment matters. The contacts for the 1996–98 round are given in HEFCE Circular 26/95, and for the 1998–2000 round in HEFCE Circular 3/97.

If you are concerned with the Scottish or Welsh systems, there is similar literature obtainable from the respective funding councils (HEFCW, 1996; SHEFC, 1997).

Quality in higher education – history and development

Accountability in higher education

Higher education in the UK is subject to accountability in every aspect of educational provision. The outcomes of such accountability have a real impact on the image and ultimately the income of departments and institutions.

At present there is a wide range of quality assurance mechanisms that maintain and enhance quality of educational provision in higher education institutions. These include the following.

Internal

The institution's internal procedures, at institutional, faculty, departmental, programme and individual staff level. These can include such things as programme validation and review boards, student feedback, peer review and staff appraisal.

External

There are five major external quality assurance mechanisms:

- quality audit
- quality assessment
- research assessment
- external examiner system
- professional accreditation.

The internal mechanisms also feature in the external processes. For example, one entire aspect of quality assessment (quality assurance and enhancement) focuses on the effectiveness of the internal mechanisms. In fact many of the internal mechanisms have evolved in response to the external scrutiny.

External examiners and accreditation by professional bodies have been the main external quality assurance mechanisms until recently (apart from the Council for National Academic Awards (CNAA) in the 'new university' sector) and tended to focus on the student assessment process and curriculum content. Quality audit, assessment and the research assessment exercise are the recent manifestations of the cult of accountability which spread throughout public services in the late 1980s and early 1990s. Together they monitor the quality of virtually every activity in higher education.

Quality audit

Quality audit was introduced by the Committee of Vice-Chancellors and Principals (CVCP) in October 1990, in response to calls from government for greater accountability in higher education (Gordon and Partington, 1993, 1995; HEQC, 1994b). The CVCP established the Academic Audit Unit (AAU) to conduct quality audits and to ensure that institutions have effective quality assurance and quality control systems. Institutions 'invited' the AAU to conduct an audit, supplying a range of briefing documents about their quality assurance policies and procedures in terms of:

- the design and review of programmes of study
- teaching, learning and the student experience
- the performance and development of academic staff
- student assessment and degree classification
- promotional material
- feedback and verification systems.

A team of academic auditors and an audit secretary from the AAU analysed the documentation and spent three days at the institution. A report was prepared in consultation with the university, whose property it remained. The cycle time for audit is six years (Gordon and Partington, 1993) and the HEQC is just completing the first round of audits, bringing the number of visits to 235 since the AAU was established.

In May 1992, the CVCP established the Higher Education Quality Council (HEQC). One of its three divisions, the Division of Quality Audit, took over the work of the AAU and now has the task of conducting academic quality audits of institutions. These audit reports, like the quality assessment reports, are available to the public.

In April 1997, following complaints about duplication and costs the audit and quality assessment processes were combined under a new Quality Assurance Agency which has taken over the functions of the HEQC and the quality assessment functions of the participating funding councils (Joint Planning Group, 1996).

Introduction and development of HEFCE quality assessment

Quality audit investigates whether an institution has appropriate quality assurance mechanisms in place and whether they are working effectively. When the 'new universities' were funded by the Polytechnics and Colleges Funding Council (PCFC), they were subject to external assessment by the CNAA. Former Universities Funding Council (UFC) institutions were not subject to such external scrutiny and thus were effectively autonomous and funding for teaching had no link to the quality of their performance. The main forms of external assessment in this sector were such things as external examiners and accreditation by professional bodies.

The first move towards public accountability for funding was the research assessment exercise, introduced in 1989. Performance could be measured by numbers of publications and research grants awarded accordingly. Originally it only influenced a minor proportion of a relatively small part of an institution's funding income.

It became inevitable that attention would turn to the lion's share of institutions' activity and funding – the teaching. The government felt that there was still a need for assessment of the actual educational provision. The claim that 'you can't measure teaching quality' was soon swept aside. In the Further and Higher Education Act of 1992 (Section 70) the government legislated that the HEFCE should:

> 'secure that provision is made for assessing the quality of education provided in institutions for whose activities it provides, or is considering providing, financial support under this part of the Act.'

In fulfilling this legislative obligation, HEFCE was left to decide on its approach to assessment aided through consultation with institutions and a number of pilot assessments. The main obligations on the funding council were set out by the (then) Secretary of State in his inaugural letter to the chairman of the HEFCE:

> 'The Council will need, in particular, to ensure that the outcomes of assessment visits are in a form which can be used to inform funding allocations. Reports of visits should be published. The Council should seek to ensure that serious shortcomings identified in reports are addressed by institutions, and monitored by the Council.'

The first assessment method designed to meet these requirements operated between February 1993 and June 1995 and focused on the educational provision within a subject rather than within a department, school or faculty (HEFCE, 1993). The subjects covered were Anthropology, Applied Social Work, Architecture, Business and Management, Chemistry, Computer Science/Studies, English, Environmental Studies, Geography, Geology, History, Law, Mechanical Engineering, Music, and Social Policy and Administration. Under this method each institution was asked to submit a self-assessment of its provision in the subject under scrutiny. This had to include a clear statement of the subject aims and objectives and an evaluation of the provision.

The onus was on the subject provider to judge the quality of their provision on a three-point scale of unsatisfactory, satisfactory or excellent. Some claims of excellence were rejected but those that were sustained were followed up by a visit. In addition, visits were made to a sample of institutions making 'satisfactory' claims and some where there was potential 'quality at risk'. Visits were carried out by teams of subject specialist assessors led by a reporting assessor. Two reports were produced; one was confidential to the funding council and the institution visited, and the second was a public document providing an account of provision.

The methodology was reviewed at the end of 1993. Opinion was canvassed from heads of HEFCE and Department of Education of Northern Ireland (DENI) funded institutions. The review included monitoring and evaluation of assessment visits and outcomes and feedback from institutions on the process and conduct of assessment as well as external evaluation by the Centre for Higher Education Studies (CHES, 1994). This resulted in a number of modifications for the next round of assessments, including a move to universal visiting, graded profiles, threshold judgement and a single public report. The overall coordination and implementation of the HEFCE quality assessment methodology is the responsibility of HEFCE's Quality Assessment Division (QAD).

The purpose of the current HEFCE quality assessment

The purposes of quality assessment currently defined by HEFCE (Circular 39/94) are:

(a) To secure value from public investment:
  (i) By ensuring that all education for which the HEFCE provides funding is of approved quality, and by encouraging speedy rectification of major shortcomings in the quality of education.
  (ii) By using quality assessment judgements to inform funding.
(b) To encourage improvements in the quality of education through the publication of assessment reports and subject overview reports, and through the sharing of best practice.
(c) To provide, through the publication of reports, effective and accessible public information on the quality of the education for which the HEFCE provides funding (HEFCE, 1994c).

The link of outcomes to funding a(ii) was reaffirmed in relation to unsatisfactory provision. The possible link between funding and quality beyond the threshold level remains under review (HEFCE, 1995f). Funding is already available for institutions to capitalize on quality assessment outcomes in the form of HEFCE's Fund for the Development of Teaching and Learning (FDTL). This fund, announced in HEFCE Circular 29/95, aims to stimulate developments in teaching and learning and to maximize involvement of institutions in the take-up and implementation of good teaching and learning practice. In the phase two funding for the 1995–96 round applicants were required to have quality approved status in the relevant unit of assessment and grade 4 in the aspect for which funding was sought.

Quality assessment in Welsh and Scottish higher education

The Welsh and Scottish higher education sectors went through a similar process of development; in fact the Welsh and English adopted a common approach at the pilot stage. The Higher Education Funding Council for Wales (HEFCW) published its statement of the arrangements for securing the assessment of quality of higher education from October 1994 onwards in HEFCW Circular W94/36HE. It confirmed the basis for its methodology: 'fitness for purpose'; prime responsibility residing with the institution; and respect for institutional mission, aims and objectives. Ahead of the single Quality Assurance Agency, it moved towards close alignment between institutions' own internal review procedures and the external processes of the HEFCW (Gordon and Partington, 1995).

Following the pilot stage the Scottish Higher Education Funding Council (SHEFC) also commissioned a report in 1993, the outcomes of which were circulated to all Scottish HEIs, for incorporation in the 1994–95 programme of assessments. Further minor developments took place for 1995–96.

It is worth mentioning quality assessment in further education (FEFC, 1993), which has a number of interesting features. It is conducted on a four-yearly visit cycle with annual submission of self-assessments. The main features – self-assessment, visit and report – are common to all UK higher and further education sectors, and there are examples of good practice to be found in its operational and procedural guidelines, from which higher education can learn. It has a detailed list of the sources of evidence that can be used in assessing provision (see Chapter 2).

The relationship between audit and assessment

Some have regarded audit and assessment as duplication of effort, but *there is no real overlap* or duplication between audit and assessment – they are different processes. Quality audit looks at an institution's *procedures* for measuring, assuring and enhancing the quality of provision, whereas quality assessment looks at the *outcomes* of applying such structures and procedures to the provision and actually measures the quality achieved. These are distinct functions as can be seen by analogy with student assessment. Quality audit corresponds to an audit of the procedures an institution has in place for measuring the quality of learning of its students, for example examination regulations, examination boards, appeals procedures, examination schedules, validity and reliability of assessment, etc. Quality assessment corresponds to the actual measurement of the student achievement, the extent of achievement of educational objectives and the means by which achievement is enhanced.

A further distinction between audit and assessment is that the first is at the institutional level and the other at subject level. Distinct though they may be, there was still a feeling that two quality systems could not be sustained and this has led to merging both audit and assessment under the QAAHE.

Merger of quality audit and assessment

From April 1997 all the functions of the HEQC and the quality assessment functions of the participating funding councils will be combined in the new Quality Assurance Agency for Higher Education (QAAHE). Its objectives include:

- the promotion and maintenance of quality and standards in higher education provided by UK universities and colleges;
- the enhancement of teaching and learning and the identification and promotion of innovation and good practice;
- the provision of information and the publication of reports on quality and standards in higher education;
- the provision of advice to government as requested.

Significant here is that the QAAHE, unlike HEFCE quality assessment, concerns itself with standards. It aims to harmonize its procedures as effectively as possible with other quality systems such as professional accreditation (Joint Planning Group, 1996).

What does quality assessment mean for you?

Quality assessment has not been greeted with overwhelming enthusiasm by all stakeholders in higher education and news of an impending assessment does not always galvanize university staff into action. It is easy to see the negative side or to view quality assessment as a threat, but it can have great benefits. The close scrutiny of the educational provision that such external stimulus encourages can lead to new insights into the way things are done. It raises the profile and importance of teaching and the dissemination of good practice is encouraged. It is therefore worth taking a look at what quality assessment means in practice to the many and varied stakeholders in higher education.

Academic teaching staff

There may be some front-loaded administrative and organizational activity required, such as improved record keeping. There will be closer scrutiny of the whole range of teaching-related activities, including classroom observation, a greater focus on teaching and learning generally and increased developmental opportunities for the teacher. There will be the need for greater liaison with peers, support services and students. The extra importance attached to teaching may lead to tangible rewards – performance-related pay is sometimes awarded to staff who have taken a leading role in preparing for quality assessment.

Heads of department/subject being assessed face particular challenges in getting everyone on board, ensuring equitable distribution of workload and organizing the visit. Quality assessment will, however, provide a greater insight into the provision, enabling positive development and improvement.

Departmental support staff

Secretaries, departmental administrators and technical staff may find a lot of work coming their way. They can assist in both the preparation and the smooth running of the visit, in particular making sure all staff and students are well informed. Quality assessment can also provide great opportunities, which should receive the appropriate recognition.

Students and parents

The whole quality assessment exercise is designed to assure the quality and the enhancement of the students' educational experience. Assessors take students' views seriously and the quality assessment exercise provides an excellent opportunity for students to contribute constructively to the development of this provision. The National Union of Students recognizes the importance of the process by providing guidelines for student representatives to enable them to optimize the effectiveness of student input (Course Reps Resource Pack, NUS, 1997).

For parents and prospective students the outcomes of quality assessment, in the form of quality assessment reports, are invaluable. For just a few pounds (or free on the Web) they can obtain the reports on the institutions that interest them and learn a tremendous amount about the provision in the chosen subject. One of the authors has found the reports invaluable in helping his son decide on a music degree – a prospective student armed with the report can demonstrate an impressive knowledge of the institution. Quality assessment outcomes are already being translated into simple league tables but it pays to go beyond this and focus on the qualitative value of the reports.

Support services staff

Assessors will visit a range of support services, such as the library, computing services, careers advice and staff development. Remember that while quality assessment *is* at the subject level there is interest in all contributions to the provision, including those from central services. The quality of support services comes under scrutiny, and will figure in the assessors' view of the provision. This will result in the need for closer liaison with academic departments and will also raise the profile of the services provided.

Educational and staff developers have a particularly crucial role to play in coordinating and facilitating preparation for quality assessment, for example, setting up peer review schemes, mock assessments and so on. Central administrative personnel may be called upon to provide statistical data relating to the subject.

Institutional management

Response to quality assessment really is a case of leading from the front. The role of institutional management is crucial in raising awareness, coordinating preparation activities, setting in place the infrastructure for response and allocating resources. Management can provide leadership and encouragement, raise the profile of and rewards for teaching, and monitor progress in both the preparation for quality assessment and any follow up. Quality assessment provides opportunities to enhance and publicize the quality of the institution's provision, helping in the recruitment of students.

Employers, professional and statutory bodies (PSBs) and subject associations

These will benefit from a wealth of information about the quality of educational provision of institutions from which they recruit or with which they are associated. They may be invited to meet assessors, if they have student placements for programmes under assessment or are a member of the institution's industrial advisory body. PSBs and subject associations are invited by HEFCE to nominate assessors, and the advice of subject associations is sought on the nature, range and characteristics of their subject. There is therefore plenty of opportunity for involvement in and feedback from quality assessment (HEFCE, 1997a).

Assessors

We should not forget the quality assessment assessors themselves. They gain a wide experience and greater insight into higher education provision, which they can take back to their own institutions. They will be in a position to advise any department coming up for assessment. Currently an HEFCE funded project is being conducted by the Educational Development Service of the University of Northumbria at Newcastle, which will report on how service as an assessor has affected the practice and commitment to teaching of academic staff (HEFCE, 1997b).

Chapter 2

The quality assessment methodology and responding to it

This chapter sets out to:

- describe the quality assessment methodology
- provide suggestions for preparing for quality assessment
  - milestones
  - assembling resources
  - gathering evidence
  - action on strengths and weaknesses
  - self-assessment
  - the visit
- suggest some useful developmental activities.

The HEFCE quality assessment methodology

The general features of quality assessment

The main features of quality assessment are as follows:

- assessment of the entire educational provision;
- assessment by a combination of self- and peer review;
- assessment in the context of the subject provider's aims and objectives for the complete student learning experience;
- public assessment methodology and criteria against which judgements are made;
- self-assessment by the provider in which

  - aims and objectives are stated
  - the educational provision is described
  - additional information/data is provided as required;
- visit by an assessment team to examine evidence for the provision;
- judgement in the form of
  - a graded profile
  - threshold judgement;
- published report.

What is assessed?

In higher education quality assessment is conducted at subject level. Subjects are defined and classified by the Higher Education Statistics Agency (HESA), and there are 61 subjects in all. The term 'subject provider' is used to describe the organizational unit(s) responsible for the delivery of the subject being assessed. Any teaching on the subject provider's programmes may be assessed, even if it is serviced by another department. For the future, the new QAAHE will, where appropriate, consider the brigading of cognate subjects within an institution. This is already anticipated in the case of monotechnic institutions such as Dartington College of Arts.

For each subject, it is the *entire educational experience* that is assessed. All quality assessment systems organize this educational provision into a number of convenient categories, each of which is separately assessed and graded. For example, in the HEFCE system, for the period 1995–98 there are six *core aspects of provision*, each of which is *equally weighted* for assessment purposes:

- curriculum design, content and organization (CDCO)
- teaching, learning and assessment (TLA)
- student progression and achievement (SPA)
- student support and guidance (SSG)
- learning resources (LR)
- quality assurance and enhancement (QAE).

HEFCE publishes lists of *key features* that expand on the content of each aspect (see the Assessors' Handbook, HEFCE, 1996a). In Scotland, SHEFC categorizes subject provision into eleven *aspects* (SHEFC, 1997):

- aims and curricula
- curriculum design and review
- the teaching and learning environment
- staff resources
- learning resources

- course organization
- teaching and learning practice
- student support
- assessment and monitoring
- students' work
- output, outcomes and quality control.

HEFCW has four *elements*:

- programmes and curricula
- teaching and learning
- assessment and academic support for students
- student achievement.

HEFCW supplies an expansion of the indicative features encompassed by these (HEFCW, 1996).

For comparison, FEFC has seven *aspects*:

- responsiveness and range of provision
- governance and management
- students' recruitment, guidance and support
- teaching and the promotion of learning
- students' achievements
- quality assurance
- resources.

FEFC expands on these in the form of 'Inspection Guidelines' in FEFC Circular 93/28. Whereas all the higher education funding councils assess all aspects or elements at the subject level only, FEFC assesses five of its aspects at the institutional level, and just two (teaching and the promotion of learning, and students' achievements) at subject level.

When is it assessed?

In HEFCE quality assessment all 61 subjects are being assessed during the first eight-year cycle from 1993 to 2001. This cycle is divided into 'rounds' of one or two years during which selected groups of subjects are assessed. For example, the HEFCE Circular 20/95 (HEFCE, 1995a) gives the forward plan for the remaining rounds as listed below.

October 1996 – September 1998
16 units of assessment:
- agriculture, forestry and agricultural sciences
- food science

- mechanical, aeronautical and manufacturing engineering
- civil engineering
- electrical and electronic engineering
- general engineering
- materials technology
- building
- town and country planning and landscape
- land and property management
- American studies
- Middle Eastern and African studies
- East and South Asian studies
- history of art, architecture and design
- communication and media studies
- drama, dance and cinematics

October 1998 – September 2000
13 units of assessment:
- medicine
- dentistry
- veterinary medicine
- anatomy and physiology
- pharmacology and pharmacy
- molecular biosciences
- organismal biosciences
- nursing
- other studies allied to medicine
- physics and astronomy
- psychology
- mathematics, stastics and operational research
- art and design

October 2000 – December 2001
11 units of assessment:
- hospitality, leisure, recreation, sport and tourism
- librarianship and information management
- business management
- economics
- politics
- classics and ancient history
- Celtic studies
- archaeology
- philosophy
- theology and religious studies
- education

The last two rounds are affected by the move to the QAAHE in April 1997 (HEFCE, 1997a). The methods, procedures and timetables as published in HEFCE Circulars 39/94, 26/95 and 11/96 will continue unchanged until

September 1998, the end of the current round, and will not be affected by the transfer to the new agency. The subjects in subsequent rounds remain as stated above but by then there may be changes to the quality assessment process.

Who does the assessing?

In higher education assessors are largely drawn from the ranks of senior or experienced teaching staff. Under the HEFCE system individual teachers may be nominated as assessors by their institution, professional bodies or subject association. Staff may also apply directly. There are two types of assessor: contract and subject specialist.

Contract assessors

Contract assessors assist in the selection and training of subject specialist assessors but their main role as the *reporting assessor* is to lead an assessment team on an assessment visit. This involves preparation for the visit, liaising with the institution, coordinating the work of subject specialist assessors, assuring the quality and nature of the evidence gathered and judgement reached, providing oral feedback on completion of the visit and coordinating the preparation of the report. The majority of contract assessors are independently contracted, with the rest seconded from HEIs. Over a third have professorial status. The reporting assessor will not normally be a specialist in the subject being assessed, and therefore is able to stand back and give a more generic view of the assessment (HEFCE, 1997b).

Subject specialist assessors

The main role of a subject specialist assessor is to participate in an assessment team as an external peer reviewer of the quality of an institution's provision in a specific subject. Details of the number and background of subject specialist assessors may be found in the HEFCE *Report on Quality Assessment 1995–96*. Most are institutional nominees, and the remainder chosen from independent applications. Because of the increasing profile of quality assessment, a higher proportion of good calibre applications has allowed HEFCE to be more selective in its choice of assessors for the coming round of assessments (HEFCE, 1997b).

By now all institutions will have a fair number of assessors in the various subjects already assessed. If you talk to those in your institution they will tell you about their intensive three to four day training. They are experienced academics, with a brief training in the quality assessment methodology, who learn most of their trade 'on the job' as assessors. As 'poachers turned game-keepers', they are ideally suited to assessing your provision – they know all the tricks but they are also likely to be tolerant and understanding of the realities of your situation.

The training of assessors is continually evolving. It tries to emulate the structure of an assessment visit, following preparatory work analysing a self-assessment. The course involves simulation and role play. There used to be a great emphasis on teaching observation, but this has now been reduced in favour of a more equitable treatment of all six aspects. The gathering and evaluation of evidence, use of the *Assessors' Handbook* and determination of grades have also all been strengthened. The training is carried out by the Universities' and Colleges' Staff Development Agency (UCoSDA), Quality Assessment Division staff and contract assessors. UCoSDA now markets some of the training materials, including videos of sample teaching sessions (UCoSDA and Loughborough University, 1996).

Training of the contract assessors is, understandably, more extensive than that of the subject specialist assessors. It includes, in addition to a specialist assessor training course, a workshop on managing visits and visit outcomes, the shadowing of an experienced reporting assessor on an assessment, and a number of other activities such as IT training and debriefing sessions.

HEFCE's QAD monitors and evaluates visits and the feedback they receive suggests that the assessors' training is a good preparation for their peer evaluation role in quality assessment.

How does the assessment work?

The subject provider is asked to describe and evaluate the quality of their provision in a self-assessment document. This sets the scene for the assessors to plan their assessment strategy, including the visit and their subsequent reporting. The funding bodies publish procedures and guidelines to help with such things as preparation of self-assessments, visits and description of provision.

A common underlying principle is that everyone is assessed against their own aims and objectives, which is a recognition of the diversity of mission in further and higher education. You then have to describe how your provision meets the aims and objectives, provide evidence of this and on the quality of provision. You are 'graded' according to the assessors' judgement of the extent to which your provision meets the aims and objectives. This is a crucial factor in the assessment process – you are not being judged in relation to other providers, but on how well you do what you say you do. HEFCE does not 'assess' the aims and objectives themselves, other than for clarity, but these are published verbatim in the quality assessment reports. HEFCE has noticed that aims and objectives are steadily improving in quality as a result of the policy of publishing them!

All evaluation of provision must be supported by evidence available to the assessors. A senior mathematician was heard to scoff at the HEFCE quality assessment – 'you now have to *prove* everything you say about your teaching'. Why should a mathematician find this strange? The gathering and presentation of evidence is crucial to the quality assessment process and forms a large part of this book. The sources of evidence will be explored by assessors through scrutiny of advance documentation and the visit.

The funding council arranges for designated assessors to visit the institution for a specified period on a timetable agreed in advance with the institution. The self-assessment is used as a guide to structure the visit. Assessors look into the whole range of provision at institutional and subject level, gathering evidence to inform their judgements. They look at a wide range of documentation, both before and during the visit; they talk to staff and students, undertake classroom observation and meet with selected individuals and groups. They also look at departmental facilities and accommodation.

Judgements about provision are informed by the self-assessment and visit, based on published criteria. The assessment team reports their final decision to the provider at the end of the visit (except in the Scottish system), and a public report is published within a few months.

All quality assessment with which we are concerned follows these broad principles. The specific details of the current HEFCE system are listed below.

- Assessment of educational provision, by subject area, of all institutions which it funds, by self-assessment and visit.
- Taught programmes at all levels of study are assessed.
- Assessment by peer review (peers with three to four days training).
- Assessment against subject provider's aims and objectives.
- Six aspects of educational provision.
- Self-assessment document (approximately 20 pages) and three to four day visit based on the self-assessment.
- Judgement in terms of a graded profile (1–4 point scale for each of the six aspects).
- One public report is issued following the assessment visit.
- A grade 1 in one or more aspects leads to reassessment within a year.
- Funding is withdrawn in whole or in part if provision is unsatisfactory after reassessment (HEFCE, 1994c)

Representation to the Council

The HEFCE system allows for a few limited forms of representation on some aspects of this methodology. Certainly, you can have some influence over the final team selected for the visit, if you have good evidence that any of the nominated team are not suitable. Examples of successful objections to team members include gender balance, conflict of interest and size of team (University Council of Modern Languages, 1996). During the visit you can also raise concerns with the reporting assessor, who should accommodate any reasonable request or complaint. Thus, if the conduct of an assessor is felt to be inappropriate, this may be raised with the assessment team or reported directly to HEFCE. If the issue is very serious, you could make a complaint to HEFCE and argue for a revisit.

There is also a procedure to make representation if one or more profile elements is graded 1. (Refer to Annex E of HEFCE Circular 26/95, should the unthinkable occur.)

What happens after the assessment?

This varies between fundings councils, but you can be sure *something* will happen. This can range from capitalizing on what you have learnt about your provision in order to develop it, to possible financial penalties or benefits depending on the funding council's policy. As yet, there is no formal follow up of any kind to higher education quality assessment – until the next cycle in a given subject. When all institutions in a given subject have been assessed, the outcomes are summarized in a *subject overview report*; these reports are a rich source of useful information.

Remember that the first thing the assessors are likely to ask in the next cycle of assessment is how effectively you responded to the outcomes of your current assessment. FEFC and HEFCW are better at encouraging follow up – in the former annual reviews are conducted and in the latter institutions have to state what developments they have made and their future plans for improvement.

The most immediate and significant impact of the assessment will probably be on your external image, and your own self-esteem. The outcomes of quality assessment are published, scores will be totted up, and league tables are already emerging. Naturally, prospective students, parents and employers will be interested in your graded profile (wouldn't you be?) A good profile will boost your confidence and pride in your provision, while a poor result...

Finally, your council funding may be affected. Certainly, if your provision falls below a certain threshold level, part or all of your funding may be removed in that subject area. More positively, there are extra funds to promote excellence. For example, in 1994–95 SHEFC awarded an extra £2 million (out of a total budget of £350m) to subject providers rated excellent. There is little doubt that eventually there will be a more formal link between quality assessment outcomes and funding.

Preparing for quality assessment

What needs to be done?

This will depend on your state of preparedness, ie the extent to which your provision demonstrably meets your subject aims and objectives. It may be that your provision is already excellent, and all you have to do is write the self-assessment and assemble the evidence for the visit. However, experience suggests that few providers are so comfortably placed. When putting the self-assessment together, most of us uncover issues that need attending to in preparation for the visit. In the rest of this chapter we run through the things to consider in preparing for quality assessment from scratch. Most of the rest of the book is then devoted to providing support for this.

When should you start preparing for quality assessment?

As soon as possible! External scrutiny of provision is here to stay, so you will be assessed. Often much of the work for quality assessment consists of putting in place quality assurance and enhancement systems and getting the documentation right. You should be doing this anyway, so ensure that systems are in place well before the assessment if possible. There is no reason why an annual self-assessment should not be an ongoing part of your quality assurance mechanisms – this is the system used by FEFC and encouraged by HEFCW.

Another reason for starting preparation early is the need to harmonize quality assessment requirements with such things as accreditation by professional bodies or internal reviews. You will also need time to generate evidence from completed cycles of evaluation and development, ie have time to assess provision, respond to weaknesses, monitor improvements and feed back into the provision.

Preparation schedule

The schedule for preparation for quality assessment can be fixed once the submission date for the self-assessment and the visit date are known, but you do not have to wait for this. Remember to take account of examination periods, vacations and the availability of other departments involved. The self-assessment will probably need to go through a number of iterations, so build this into the schedule.

Preparation for the visit can be done in parallel with the self-assessment document. In fact, it is best to use the self-assessment preparation as the basis for preparing for the visit. The self-assessment is an account and evaluation of what you do – what you do well, and not so well – and you will need to address the weaker areas. For example, a visit in January may mean that the last chance to do anything relating to student assessment is before the summer term examinations of the previous year. This would have to be built into the schedule.

The milestones

So far, preparation for quality assessment is a novel experience for every subject provider. It can be an invigorating experience – a whole new language to learn, increased interaction between students and staff and an opportunity for good practice to be rewarded. But because few have the time to enjoy it, reaction to quality assessment varies greatly – some see it as a thorough nuisance. Others will take it seriously and relish the chance to show off their wares.

The milestones in the preparation for quality assessment are as follows.

- Identify roles and responsibilities (this chapter).
- Raise awareness and keep everyone informed (this chapter).
- Assemble resources for preparation (this chapter).
- Gather evidence and identify strengths and weaknesses (this chapter and Chapters 4–9).
- Action planning to address weaknesses and disseminate strengths (Chapters 4–9).
- Prepare the self-assessment document (Chapter 3).
- Prepare and coordinate the visit (Chapter 10).

These activities require input from a range of people at all levels in the institution and need some organization.

Roles and responsibilities

Getting people on board

This can be a difficult task, but once people are roped in they tend to appreciate quite quickly the potential value of the exercise. There are, however, endless opportunities for displacement activity or for throwing in the towel in despair – anything to avoid the awesome task of actually doing something about it. All subject staff need to be involved in the process – the more proactive the response the more influence can be exerted on the visit and the outcome. After all, the assessors are chosen from the ranks of university staff themselves and will usually be keen to work with the provider. The head of department and other senior staff have particularly important roles in getting people involved.

In the Welsh system, a quality assessment manager is assigned to an institution, and if possible manages all the subject assessments for that institution.

He or she provides advice on all aspects of quality assessment, including the self-assessment and organization of the visits. The quality assessment manager also rationalizes the process to avoid duplication of assessment of elements of the visit that are common to all subjects.

Many people complain about the amount of time needed for preparation for quality assessment, on top of preparation for such things as RAE and accreditation. It is true that the pressures on institutions are immense, but somehow time must be found for response to quality assessment: it is one of the most important issues an institution faces. For many institutions it is essentially assessing some 70–80% of their activity (RAE impacts on say 20–30% in most cases) and the outcomes are publicly available. A related objection is that it is just an exercise in paperwork. Certainly, the 'mountain of paperwork' cry has some resonance, but it shouldn't be overdone. It is not really onerous when considering that it represents your whole provision. Much of it, such as minutes of meetings, student questionnaires and so on should already be available. The self-assessment itself is only about 20 pages, which is hardly encyclopaedic.

Many staff are unduly influenced by horror stories about quality assessment related by colleagues in assessed departments. Most of these are associated with the first rounds of quality assessment which were more primitive. Things have improved since and HEFCE and the new QAAHE have good reason to ensure that they continue to improve. There will still be problems, but we simply have to live with and learn from them.

Subject and institutional structures for response to quality assessment

It is sensible to set up a group to coordinate local preparation activities at the subject or departmental level. The group must have authority and experience in the provision being assessed and be familiar with the quality assessment process. It may coopt staff who already have experience of being assessed or assessors from other subjects. Quality assessment is too important to assign duties solely on the basis of availability or current workload; the best people should be used, even if this means having to shift other duties around. In addition to such a coordinating group, all subject staff (including support staff) should have some role in the preparation. For example, depending on the number of staff available, a small group could be set up for each of the core aspects.

As well as coordinating the departmental response, the group can also set up communication links to liaise with the other contributors to the provision; for example, servicing academic departments, the library, schools liaison and other support services. The group can also coordinate preparation of the self-assessment. In order to maximize input to the visit, the chair of the group could be the subject contact liaising directly with the HEFCE. There may already be such a group in place, in the form of a teaching committee for example. It is desirable that this is coordinated centrally, at institutional level.

It is often the case that a number of subjects in an institution are being assessed at the same time. It makes sense to pull these together and prepare in parallel. This facilitates exchange of good practice, spreads the workload, provides mutual support and enables a united approach to central support services.

The growing importance of quality and standards in higher education is already causing many HEIs to establish bodies to deal with these at the institutional level. These may be watchdog committees or facilitating units whose job it is to help departments prepare for quality assessment and audit. Some institutions might establish a high ranking office, say at pro-vice chancellor level, to oversee quality matters. The point of such institutional-level structures is to give the highest profile to legislative requirements such as quality assessment; to coordinate and facilitate related institution-wide activities; and to gather and disseminate good practice.

Some suggested responsibilities

Specific individual responsibilities to consider are as follows.

Subject contact
HEFCE actually require a named contact for liaison on quality assessment.

Self-assessment author
It is advisable to have a single author, who coordinates and pulls together contributions from others.

Quality assessment secretary
Duties to include administration, researching, organizing and disseminating information.

An aspect coordinator for each aspect
A named member of staff responsible for the coordination of activities and maximizing the grade for the aspect.

Support department liaison
To coordinate liaison with support departments such as the library and computing services. Or this role could be shared by the coordinators for the learning resources (LR) aspect and the student support and guidance (SSG) aspect.

Quality assessment awareness officer
A key role is keeping everyone informed of progress on quality assessment preparation.

External liaison
To liaise with external bodies or individuals as appropriate, such as relevant PSBs, employers and alumni.

And don't forget the students! They should be involved in quality assessment from the start. Students can help to prepare the self-assessment, formulate the teaching, *learning* and assessment strategy and assist during the visit. They will be interviewed by the assessors and will need to be briefed about this. If the Students' Guild has an officer responsible for educational training and development, get them involved too.

If your subject is vocational, your professional association can be helpful in the quality assessment process. It can set the context of your programme in the general professional environment out in the real world. Similarly, as mentioned in Chapter 1, PSBs and subject associations may be involved in quality assessment by HEFCE from the outset and can help to set the scene for the assessment of that subject. Liaise with them if they are relevant to your provision.

Raise awareness and keep everyone informed

Tell everybody about it!

Keep everyone informed by taking proactive, speedy action to disseminate all information relating to quality assessment. Provide pithy digests of the official documents, such as HEFCE Circular 39/94, along with pointers about what it means for the staff involved. Senior management can assist in dissemination by talking to departments, describing the institutional context and the implications of quality assessment. Information can also be distributed widely through newsletters, e-mail and electronic bulletin boards.

The institution should aim to ensure that all staff know and understand the main features of the quality assessment exercise and appreciate its importance to the institution. They should understand their role in the process and be both sympathetic and proactive in supporting the institution's and the subject provider's response. It is worthwhile keeping staff up to date on other issues in higher education, such as the new QAAHE, HEQC's work on graduate standards and the outcomes of the forthcoming Dearing Review. Staff should be as informed as the assessors.

Service and support departments need to be kept informed about progress in quality assessment. Again distil and interpret HEFCE literature and highlight the information that is specifically relevant to them. Brief them on the questions they might be asked by assessors. This is best coordinated at the institutional level since support departments may be involved in a number of assessments.

Translate 'HEFCE speak'

What a fuss is made about this! Academics who delight in masses of detailed technical jargon baulk at a few vaguely technical terms used in quality assessment literature. Some of the terms may sound pompous and unnecessary; for example, isn't a 'subject provider' just a fancy term for 'department'? No, it simply recognizes that sometimes the input to a particular subject may come from a number of sources that are not easily identified with a single department. On the other hand, there may be two or more subject areas assessed separately in a single department.

Some HEFCE terms are poorly defined, such as 'aims' and 'objectives'. All you can do is interpret them as best you can (see Chapter 3). Other phrases are open to a range of interpretations, such as 'transferable skills' and 'student learning experience'. Some HEFCE terms have an everyday use that might confuse, for example 'aspect of provision'. This is a specifically defined part of your total provision but you often want to use 'aspect' simply to refer to a particular part of the provision located within a specific HEFCE 'aspect'.

Yet another problem is that accreditation or institutional bodies may have a different terminology to quality assessment. For modular provision you have an opportunity to clarify the terminology in an annex to the self-assessment.

Assemble resources for preparation – a quality assessment resource pack

Here we refer to material and resources for the preparation itself, not the evidence required to support your evaluation of the provision, which we discuss in later chapters. A considerable amount of material that could be useful in preparing for quality assessment includes funding council documentation, sample self-assessments, quality assessment reports, assessors' *aide-mémoires* and feedback from assessed departments.

It is useful to put together a resource pack of such material, preferably at the institutional level, by a central unit responsible for coordinating the institution's response to quality assessment. The resource can be regularly updated and made available to departments preparing for assessment. The pack should inform users about the quality assessment process, the experience of quality assessment at the institution and guidelines for preparation. It should evolve over time and can become a running commentary on quality assessment at your institution, documenting lessons learnt and good practice identified. Below we list some of the things you might include in the pack, for HEFCE quality assessment.

HEFCE documentation
- C14/94 Units for the Assessment of the Quality of Education
- C20/95 The Forward Programme for Quality Assessment
- C26/95 Quality Assessment between October 1996 and September 1998
- *Assessors' Handbook 1996–98.*

Feedback on quality outcomes
- quality assessment reports
- subject overview reports
- reports on quality assessment 1992–95 and 1995–96.

Quality assessment at your institution
- timetable of visits for subjects in your institution
- quality assessment at your institution – outcomes, lessons learnt and good practice
- self-assessment documents and quality assessment reports for all providers in your institution.

Preparation for quality assessment
This will include such things as guidelines for writing the self-assessment and prepara-tion for the visit. Examples might include:
- summary sheet of the aspects and key features of provision, assessors' *aide-mémoires*, etc
- guide to writing a self-assessment document, including writing aims and objectives
- documentation on central services such as the library and computing services.

You might also include in the resource pack proformas and other documentation for recording progress, meetings, lessons learnt during the actual preparation for quality assessment.

Example proformas
- organizational infrastructure for quality assessment preparation (who does what)
- personal action plans and schedule for quality assessment preparation, ie record of individual responsibilities and progress
- aspect action plan for quality assessment preparation – plan and record for identify-ing and addressing strengths and weaknesses in the provision.

It may appear that all this is adding to the paperwork, but done properly it is just good record keeping. In preparation for quality assessment much is learnt and often just as quickly forgotten in the hurly-burly of condensing it all into the self-assessment. The proformas are intended to facilitate prepara-tion and record lessons learnt. They should help in gathering the evidence, compiling the self-assessment, preparing for the visit and as evidence under quality assurance and enhancement.

Remember that quality assessment is changing rapidly and staff need to keep up to date. When learning from the experience of departments which have been assessed, keep this in mind. We have found it best to customize resources to the mode of operation of the department preparing for assessment. Where departments assign staff to particular aspects it is useful to have a resource pack per aspect. Each provides a description of the aspect, including key features, a grid to gather evidence (see page 30), what assessors say at the national level and in the institution, and a proforma for writing the self-assessment.

If you haven't done so already, this might be the time to set up a departmental teaching and learning resource room or library, containing literature and records relating to teaching and learning. This is becoming increasingly important to support new staff, capture rapidly disappearing expertise and experience and to inform all staff of new educational developments.

Tools for assessing the provision

The AIDE-MÉMOIRE and key issues for the aspects

The fact that the self-assessment is so short indicates the need to be systematic and organized in writing it. It is difficult to keep in mind the plethora of things that you have to describe, the many different sources of evidence to be gathered and to match them up. We need a systematic approach to this and to assembling evidence for the visit. One approach we have found useful in practice is to identify within each aspect a number of key issues that are likely to arise in the quality assessment; these are distilled from the Quality Assessment *aide-mémoire* given in Annexe A of the *Assessors' Handbook* (HEFCE, 1996a) from analysis of the quality assessment outcomes to date, and from similar *aide-mémoires* used by the other funding councils. We also categorize the various sources of evidence that are available, and then match these sources against the key issues in each aspect in an 'issues/evidence' grid, linking sources of evidence to the issues on which they can provide information.

The *aide-mémoire* has been described as 'the bible' by a number of assessors (but some have been less complimentary). It covers most of the issues they need to focus on and provides a checklist for systematically assessing provision. You might almost think of the *aide-mémoire* as the examination paper – and you can get a copy in advance! Time pressures during the visit are likely to encourage assessors to stick mainly to the *aide-mémoire*. We understand that it can be customized to the nature of an institution and is likely to evolve under the new QAAHE (indeed, the number of aspects could be reduced, with a corresponding redistribution of the material). This is one reason we have not always adhered strictly to the *aide-mémoire* questions given in the *Assessors' Handbook*. Instead, we have compiled a set of key issues which we hope is sufficiently generic to be durable, while remaining incisive and rigorous. The issues we have itemized form the basis for the aspect chapters (Chapters 4–9).

Of course, the *aide-mémoire* will not prevent inspired assessors ad-libbing their way into your darkest secrets, so be prepared for surprises. And don't be satisfied with our version, or the funding council's – design your own, incorporating specific features of your own provision. We have tried to work out what sort of issues will arise during an assessment of your provision. The idea of the key issues is simply to focus your thoughts on particular areas and to provide a rough framework, not to turn the exercise into one of ticking boxes. It helps to bring some element of organization into what is sometimes a rather messy exercise. The issues are only prompts, any one of which may spark off further ideas about your provision; you then have to assemble supporting evidence relating to the various issues. Remember that all of this is not only for the self-assessment writer – all staff and students could be quizzed by the assessors, and should be prepared to comment on appropriate issues.

Sources of evidence

The sources of evidence are many and varied; below is an illustrative sample to which you can add your own. For more ideas see the *Specification for a Quality Management Framework at Departmental Level* produced by the Engineering Professors' Council (Burge *et al.*, 1996). This lists about 70 sources of evidence that a typical provider might draw on. (If you think that is impressive, take a look at the FEFC Circular 97/12 (FEFC, 1997), which contains some 170 sources.) We have grouped our comparatively modest sources into five categories.

1. *Institutional – external*
   HEQC audit
   accreditation
   external examiner
   alumni
   employers
   PSBs
   quality assessment

2. *Institutional – internal*
   approval and validation boards/committees

departmental literature such as the Student Handbook
registry and planning departments
library and information services
careers service
Schools Liaison
Students' Guild
staff development
appraisal outcomes

3. *Performance indicators*
   examination and coursework results
   cohort analysis
   entry qualifications
   staff CVs
   management information statistics

4. *Student feedback*
   staff/student committees
   student questionnaires
   structured student interviews
   students' work

5. *Peer evaluation*
   classroom observation
   examination moderation and monitoring
   staff peer review reports

Each of these sources may provide various types of information on a range of issues. It is important to ensure the validity and reliability of the evidence they yield.

Much of the evidence to be gathered will be documentary, and getting this together can be a trial. However, there are steps you can take to reduce the burden.

- Use documents that already exist where possible.
- Use originals, rather than copies, including student work.
- Liaise with relevant administrators well in advance regarding the required documentation.
- Learn from previous assessments.
- Appoint one person with the responsibility for coordinating and gathering the information.
- Prepare a list of documents and send to all relevant staff, well in advance, so there is sufficient time to gather and evaluate the necessary information.
- Ensure all the documents are named and recognized by all staff involved.

Issues/evidence grid

We can match the issues against the available sources of evidence in an issues/evidence grid. Where a given source can provide evidence on a given issue we can record whether the source indicates a strength or a weakness, and other points of interest. As a simple example, the grid below indicates the matching of just four sources of evidence (accreditation documentation, external examiners' reports, student questionnaires, and classroom observation by a peer) against three typical issues (vocational relevance of the curriculum, classroom delivery of a lecturer X and match of student assessment to learning objectives).

	Accreditation	External examiner	Student questionnaire	Peer observation
Vocational relevance	S	S		
Teaching by X			S	W
Assessment against objectives		S		

Here, evidence on vocational relevance can be obtained from accreditation and the external examiner (provided they are asked) and the sources indicate that this is a strong area. Student questionnaires and classroom observation, in this case, tell us nothing about vocational relevance. On the other hand, they can both tell us something about X's teaching and here they seem to disagree – clearly the peer and X need to get together to discuss any deficiencies observed. On the assessment issue only the external examiner can provide evidence and a strength is indicated.

This approach can be as detailed as you wish. It enables you to select sources of evidence in an efficient and systematic way; for example, for each issue you need to have a couple of sources, for cross-reference purposes, and you may find that some sources can give you information on a wide range of issues. It also helps in identifying ways in which you can extend the scope of the sources of evidence, for example, the students might be asked for their views on vocational relevance, or the accrediting body could be asked to comment on the assessment issue. The approach can also reveal gaps in evidence, showing where you might need to seek additional sources to cover all your provision.

Action on strengths and weaknesses

The issues/evidence grid enables a more structured analysis of your strengths and weaknesses. Once you have completed the grid the next stage will be to gather the sources of evidence, prioritize weaknesses identified and consider how they may be addressed. Of course, you will want to consolidate and disseminate your strengths.

Weaknesses identified may be:

- dealt with before the self-assessment is submitted, or at least before the visit;
- mentioned in the self-assessment, along with means by which they will be addressed;
- ignored in the hope that no one picks them up (only as an absolute last resort).

Academics can be informal in dealing with issues and problems arising in teaching, using minimal record keeping and documentation. That may have been sustainable in the halcyon days of ample resources and negligible accountability, and even then we all know that many things were just not followed up. These days everyone is rushed off their feet and the quality assessment process imposes tight and unforgiving schedules. If an identified weakness is *not* addressed, the assessors are likely to spot it, which may affect their judgement of the provision. It is therefore essential to document decisions taken on which weaknesses will be addressed, how they will be addressed, who will be responsible and when they will be done. Clear time-bound action plans need to be put in place. There may not be the time or resources to address all of the problems before the visit, in which case deal with a selection of the most important and have plans for the rest. This in itself will provide evidence to present to the assessors of continual self-criticism and improvement.

Strengths are not only to be flaunted in the self-assessment; assessors will want to see them disseminated both within the department and across the institution. If, for example, your institution has been awarded funding under the FDTL initiative, make sure that you are also benefiting by sharing in the good practice it recognizes.

Much of the work on addressing weaknesses and strengths will be dealt with in the aspect chapters (Chapters 4–9); at the end of this chapter we describe some general developmental activities that are useful for any aspect of provision.

Prepare the self-assessment

Chapter 3 is devoted to the self-assessment, here we simply emphasize its role as an evaluative tool in the overall quality assessment process. The self-assessment provides a useful focus for the preparation for quality assessment. In order to put it together a clear understanding of strengths and weaknesses and how you might address them is essential. This takes time to develop, which is another argument for starting preparation as early as possible. Writing the self-assessment continually raises unexpected questions, no matter how well you think you know your provision. Sometimes it is even difficult to formulate the right questions – different versions of the *same* question come up under different aspects and you have to be alert to duplication. This requires thorough familiarity with the provision and its idiosyncrasies.

Prepare for the visit

This is dealt with in Chapter 10. You have a little more time (at least three months after the self-assessment submission) to address strengths and weaknesses. It is important that progress has been made on those flagged up in the self-assessment. In addition, there is the organization and administration of the visit itself to attend to. In the HEFCE system the judgement is delivered at the end of the visit, but this is really the beginning of the long developmental journey that quality assessment is intended to encourage.

Useful developmental activities

Not only for quality assessment

Two favourite reactions to the closer scrutiny exerted by quality assessment have been the introduction of 'mock assessment visits' and peer evaluation schemes such as 'critical friends' or 'buddies' systems involving classroom observation. These are fairly predictable responses to what appears to be the major novel component of the assessment exercise – observation of teaching during a visit, and they are relatively easy to implement. Other sensible responses would be the training and education of staff, formalized self-evaluation by staff and systematic sharing of good practice.

These are valuable developmental activities which should be ongoing in any enlightened learning organization and, indeed, many of them are virtually in place. For example, most institutions have some sort of periodic review of major aspects of their provision at departmental level, and the tendency is for them to be aligned with the quality assessment process so that they become *de facto* mock assessments. We have had forms of self-evaluation, training of staff and sharing of good practice for a long time, albeit often on an informal, ad hoc, basis. To become effective developmental tools, these only have to be systemized and formalized.

Training and education of academic staff

Training and education for teaching and learning is in its infancy in higher education. Most academic staff, including the majority of assessors, have no formal teaching qualifications. This situation is beginning to change, and will almost certainly accelerate, driven by quality assessment itself. Many universities, particularly the newer ones, now have programmes for professional development in teaching accredited by one means or another. For example, at present, the Staff and Educational Development Association (SEDA) has about 35 accredited programmes under its Teacher Accreditation Scheme, and more should follow.

As noted in Chapter 1, the HEFCE assessors are essentially experienced academics with a few days training provided by UCoSDA. Even if academic staff about to be assessed currently receive no training at all, the institution can arrange for them to be trained to a similar level to that of the assessors, so that they will at least have an insight into the assessors' background. UCoSDA has provided institutions with tailored versions of the assessors' training (at a fee) for this purpose. Also UCoSDA has published *Making the Grade* (UCoSDA and Loughborough University, 1996) which contains material used for training assessors. The material can provide the basis for an in-house staff development programme preparing staff for quality assessment.

Notice that we have been careful to mention 'education' as well as 'training'. In an educational establishment of all places, staff should be educated as well as trained. The aim should be to make staff as articulate and informed as possible in regard to teaching and its development. When applying for their post, assessors are asked to list what they consider to be the most significant changes in higher education in recent years – how would staff answer this one? Of course, you should also encourage as many members of staff as possible to become assessors and use their skills in preparation for quality assessment.

Mock assessment visits

It is unlikely that a mock assessment would have the rigour and intensity of the real thing, but it is certainly possible to cover the same ground. A subject provider could arrange one themselves internally or invite external consultants, but it is probably best organized and administered at the institutional level. The most simple approach is to adapt or extend the periodic review procedures that most institutions already have in place.

Assessors already available in the institution are naturally used to serve on mock assessments, but it is important to remember that they may have been assessors under a different system. This became particularly noticeable when pre-April 1995 assessors were used on post-April 1995 mock assessments. The whole spirit of the assessment process changed and this was evident in the criteria and judgements of the assessors. Pre-April 1995 assessors tended to look for *claims*, rather than *description* and *evaluation*, and had to relearn the quality assessment process.

Setting up a peer review scheme – classroom observation

The existence of a good internal peer review scheme sends positive messages about the importance attached to teaching. Peer review may be used, for example, to develop staff and educational provision, identify and disseminate good practice in teaching and review the introduction of new teaching methods. Peer review is most commonly associated with classroom observation, but it can encompass most of the activities involved in educational provision.

Common objections raised to classroom observation in particular are that peer observation perpetuates conformity of teaching; the behaviour of the observed is affected by the presence of the observer; and no one is qualified to comment on someone else's teaching. While there may be elements of truth in all of these, the fact remains that classes *will* be observed and assessed, so it is as well to get used to it in the presence of your own colleagues. (Unless you are in Wales – staff can formally refuse to be observed under the HEFCW system.)

In implementing a classroom observation system you could follow the model used by assessors using their training materials (UCoSDA, 1996). For the HEFCE protocol on teaching observation see Chapter 5. There is also plenty of good literature and practice on peer observation to consult and it is probably better to design your own system, to suit your own local needs (Brown *et al.*, 1993; Cox, 1994; Gibbs *et al.*, 1989; O'Neil and Pennington, 1992).

If you are going to introduce a peer observation scheme, make sure that the ground rules are agreed first:

- open, negotiated methodology
- agreement on use of outcomes
- non-judgemental but supportive
- agreement on timing and duration of observation
- agreement on what to observe and the criteria used

- pre-briefing on objectives of observed session
- debriefing in spirit of cooperation and mutual benefit.

Prior to observation you have to decide on the observer, the teaching session to be observed, and how observation will be conducted. Your 'critical friend' may be a colleague in the same subject area, a mentor, or simply a member of staff who you respect as a teacher. Critical friends can provide mutual evaluation by observing each other. If this seems too cosy, an alternative is for triads or larger teams to observe each other.

The choice of session to be observed should be a matter of negotiation between the observer and observed and will depend on the purposes of the observation. You may schedule a number of observations, so that observation is a continuous process rather than a one-off event. Fullerton (in Brown *et al.*, 1993) suggests no more than five observations a year.

The conduct of the observation should be agreed between the parties involved, for which widely accepted elements of good practice are recommended. There should always be a briefing session before the observation, at which both parties discuss the purpose of the observation and what they want to get out of it. The discussion might include criteria for evaluation, location of observer, duration of observation, contact with students, records kept and follow up. Also, agreement should be reached on what use will be made of the outcomes.

Observation checklists abound in the literature, for all types of teaching activity. Simply adopt or adapt one that fits your purposes. Such checklists are only prompts in any case, stimulating ideas for discussion during the debrief. There is much to be said for a very simple, open-ended checklist of the kind: what went well, what would you rather forget and what would you change next time? On the observer's part, they can make a strict chronological record of the session, or simply note key points that stand out, or focus on specific issues such as the start or the end of the session.

Giving feedback on the observation can be difficult and ideally the observer should be trained. The purpose of the post-observation feedback is to provide the observee with an independent view of what went on. The observer should act as a mirror, not as a judge or superior. Additionally, the observee should be given the opportunity to give their views on how the session went. While the initial discussion might be focused on the session, it may profitably be opened up into other areas of interest, exploring new ideas on teaching and learning. Also, 'critical friends' can review all aspects of each others' teaching, including teaching materials, student assessment and so on.

During debriefing the focus should be on behaviour rather than the person. Feedback should be specific, so that the observee can make use of the information. It should be given as soon as possible after the event, with a balance between positive and negative feedback, starting with the positive. All comments should be supported by evidence.

Good feedback should lead naturally to an action plan. The observee may gain a number of insights providing the motivation to change aspects of his or her existing approach. The following questions could help in action planning.

- What aspects of your teaching are you most happy with and are willing to disseminate?
- What aspects do you feel you would like to work on or improve?
- What do you need to do in order to improve in this area?
- Who might be able to help you?
- What resources do you need?
- How will you know when you have improved?

Self-evaluation

The best way to formalize self-evaluation of staff is through a teaching portfolio. Portfolios are now common practice in many professions (nurses, for example have an exceptionally good track record here; see Kenworthy and Hunt, 1993). Of course, all forms of evidence and professional record will go into the portfolio but this should merely be the raw material for continual self-evaluation and improvement. Increasingly, portfolios are being used in training courses in higher education teaching, for appraisal purposes and in promotion and job applications. Assessors are likely to be impressed if they see that it is normal for staff to keep a teaching portfolio (Cox, 1994; Gibbs, 1989; Redman, 1994; Seldin, 1997).

Dissemination of good practice

One of the early arguments against quality assessment was that teaching was too subject dependent; teaching chemical engineering was nothing like teaching French, for example. Quality assessment dispels this myth; most provision in higher education is in fact generic and subject independent. Only the CDCO aspect deals directly with the subject curriculum and much of that is generic. Classroom teaching observed in the TLA aspect would also reveal the subject area but the assessment of the aspect is still largely on generic, subject independent lines. Thus, both the observation and the students' work proforma (Annexes E and F in the *Assessors' Handbook*) are subject independent.

Since the bulk of provision is subject independent, there is plenty of opportunity for the dissemination of good practice – chemical engineering *can* learn from French and vice versa. This can be achieved by staff development workshops, publishing good practice, parallel preparation for quality assessment and so on. There should also be sharing of good practice within a subject. Assessors often point to the need to disseminate good practice between the lecturers in a subject, having observed virtually everyone teach. One of the main purposes of peer review schemes is to do precisely that.

Quality assessment itself, through its reports on outcomes, provides an excellent source of ideas and good practice on all aspects of educational provision. We recommend that every institution has copies of all quality assessment reports, in all subjects, as well as the subject overview reports and the appropriate funding council reports. For any of the issues we consider in Chapters 4–9 or indeed any issue in educational provision in higher education, the reports provide speedy access to a veritable goldmine of material.

The subject overview reports provide a starting point, summarizing the main positive features and recommendations organized into the six aspects. It is easy to follow up points of interest by delving into the individual quality assessment reports for each institution. This is a fascinating and rewarding exercise, which we predict will deeply influence the academic profession. Never before have we had such access to the national repository of expertise and experience in teaching and learning.

Chapter 3

The self-assessment

This chapter describes and discusses:

- the HEFCE self-assessment
- pointers for preparing the self-assessment
- how the self-assessment is analysed
- the HEFCE definitions relating to objectives and outcomes
- how to formulate subject aims and objectives
- writing the self-assessment.

Purpose, content and structure of the self-assessment

Purpose of the HEFCE self-assessment

The self-assessment is the document in which you describe, evaluate and substantiate your educational provision. The self-assessment provides pointers to the evidence that assessors will follow up on their visit, and to a large extent the self-assessment determines what the assessors will look for, what sorts of questions they will ask and who they will speak to. In short, it shapes the agenda for the visit. It is possible to redeem poor features of a self-assessment during the visit, but you can get off to a flying start by having a good self-assessment.

Part of the self-assessment is straightforward statistical data relating to staff profiles and programme structures. The more difficult parts relate to your subject aims and objectives and the evaluation of the core aspects of provision. Most of this chapter is devoted to the issue of aims and objectives; Chapters 4–9 deal with the six individual core aspects.

The self-assessment is also a tool for quality assurance and enhancement. The quality of the document and its use in leading to improvement in provision is assessed under the QAE aspect. Assessors welcome an evaluative, rather than a descriptive, self-assessment and evidence of improvements to provision as a result of preparing the self-assessment.

Interestingly, in their feedback to HEFCE on assessment visits, institutions and assessors expressed some reservations about the clarity of guidelines for preparing the self-assessment (given in Circular 39/94) and about its helpfulness during the visit (HEFCE, 1997b). This response was particularly strong from former PCFC institutions, where only 63 per cent agreed that 'It was evident that the self-assessment informed the enquiries made during the visit'. Certainly in putting this chapter together, we have found that the guidelines on preparation of the self-assessment are not always clear or helpful, particularly with respect to aims and objectives.

Content and structure of the self-assessment

In the self-assessment you have to identify 'the organizational unit (or units) within the institution responsible for the subject delivery', referred to as the *subject provider*. The range of taught provision within your subject should also be indicated, including all the programmes to be assessed under the subject. The self-assessment has two main sections: the *Framework*, and the *Evaluation of the Quality of Education*. There are also four optional *annexes*.

The Framework

The Framework of a self-assessment provides a context for the provision; stating the aims and objectives for the subject, data on the student and staff profile and the learning resources *made available by the institution* to support the subject under assessment. Take note of the italics: the HEFCE quality assessment method recognizes that the subject provider does not necessarily have control over all of its resources; ultimately it is the institution that determines the resourcing of a subject. In this respect it is an assessment of *the institution's* provision. A similar point may be made about the SSG and QAE aspects: while some features of these may be in your control, others will be at the institutional level.

The statement of the aims and objectives 'will preface the self-assessment, shape the assessment visit and be published in full in the assessment report' (HEFCE, 1994c). This important part of the self-assessment is often one that people find the most difficult to write – and you only have 500 words. It is not something that all university departments are used to doing and, indeed, the self-assessment may be the first occasion on which subject aims and objectives have been explicitly documented.

In the remainder of the framework you have no more than 700 words to describe the staff and student profile and itemize the learning resources, such as laboratory equipment, information technology and library provision. This is different from the *LR* aspect, in which you describe how the resources are *effectively deployed* in supporting the educational experience. This distinction is important: there should be no duplication. Stick to data in the framework and leave the use of resources to the LR aspect. For example, in the framework you may state the number of personal computers available for student use. Under the LR aspect you would describe how the students use these computers and give evidence of how effective they are in supporting student learning.

The Evaluation of the Quality of Education

In the Evaluation of the Quality of Education you describe and evaluate the quality of your provision as defined by the six aspects.

1. Curriculum design, content and organization (CDCO)
2. Teaching, learning and assessment (TLA)
3. Student progression and achievement (SPA)
4. Student support and guidance (SSG)
5. Learning resources (LR)
6. Quality assurance and enhancement (QAE)

This is the 'meat' of the self-assessment. It should not exceed 4,000 words, roughly ten pages of A4 (12-point font). This is a tight restriction, particularly if you have a large number of programmes in the same subject area. Careful planning is needed to outline the key points of the provision. It is one of the main reasons why preparation of the self-assessment needs to begin as early as possible – so you have time to shorten it! (For the Welsh self-assessment there is no word limit, which is perhaps worse.)

Annexes

There are up to four annexes all with strict page number limits.

1. Any quantitative and qualitative indicators that you currently use, including the basis for calculation, the relation to your aims and objectives and how they inform progress towards meeting them (up to five pages of A4 or 2,000 words maximum). The Council suggests including statistical indicators such as entry profile, progression and completion rates, student attainment, and employment and further study.

2. A factual description of course structures, options and pathways relevant to your subject (text, diagrams or both, up to three pages of A4 or 1,200 words maximum).
3. A description of any modular scheme of which your subject is part (text, diagrams or both, up to two pages of A4 or 800 words maximum).
4. A description of any partnerships or franchise arrangements you have with further or higher education institutions (text, diagrams or both, up to two pages of A4 or 800 words maximum).

The stipulations about word and page limits are taken very seriously by HEFCE. They scan self-assessments to check limits and hyphenation counts as two words, one word over and the self-assessment may be returned, so best not to risk it! The self-assessment will be returned if the aims and objectives are not clear enough to enable an assessment to be conducted.

General pointers for preparing the self-assessment

Begin work on the self-assessment as early as possible

The job of preparing the self-assessment is out of all proportion to its modest length. We have heard a head of department dismiss the task as 'just like writing a research grant proposal'. This is not the case. It is more like writing a research article. Everything you put in the self-assessment will be scrutinized before and during the visit. Careful forward planning is important for producing a good self-assessment. In preparing it, you are likely to uncover many issues that need clarification, dissemination or correction before the document is submitted or before the visit. You need time to implement such things; simply locating or gathering the evidence takes time. Also, some steps need to be taken in appropriate sequence; for example, the aims and objectives need to be drafted right from the start – they may 'evolve' throughout the production of the self-assessment, but some sort of starting point must be established. Other issues such as student assessment procedures need to be addressed at particular times.

Who should write the self-assessment?

Contributions to the self-assessment should reflect the breadth of interests involved. It is unlikely that any one person will have the detailed knowledge of all the aspects of provision but for coherence it is best written by an individual who collates and coordinates a team of one or more staff with responsibility for each aspect. It is useful if all staff can be involved collectively in the formulation of the aims and objectives. If a number of people contribute to the document, be careful to avoid contradictions in the text and ensure consistency of style; if they provide their contributions in bullet point form it will be easier to edit.

Involve as many people as possible in preparing the self-assessment, including support staff, staff who have been assessed, students, assessors within your institution, specialists in teaching and learning (eg staff/educational development), and central staff with an overview of the process. Students can also contribute to the preparation; indeed, assessors may ask them if they have been involved in writing the self-assessment. If they haven't been involved they should at least have seen a copy. Particularly for the SSG and LR aspects, you will also need to consult staff in central support services. If you have sandwich provision with industrial placement, or a period abroad, you may need to consult with employers or host institutions.

Style and format

There are no specific guidelines on the style and format of the self-assessment. Assessors are more likely to be concerned about how easy it is to read and understand, rather than seeing a glossy presentation. Aim for something like a manuscript submitted to a journal for publication.

Be concise and explicit, use cross-referencing and frequently *refer to your objectives*. This is particularly important – assessors have often commented on lack of reference to the aims and objectives in the body of the self-assessment. Be aware of institutional and subject 'jargon'; the reporting assessor is normally a non-subject specialist and the subject assessors are unlikely to be familiar with your institution. While you can't provide a glossary in the self-assessment because of the word limit, you could provide one to the assessment team in advance of the visit, or in the base room. Also, get your own story straight; it is not uncommon for different terms to be used for the same thing in the same self-assessment. The standard example is 'staff meeting' also being known as 'departmental meeting'.

A common fault found in self-assessments is the inclusion of description and evidence under the wrong aspect, which can easily happen because of the overlap of the aspects and the lack of guidance from HEFCE. A related problem is overlap and repetition between the different aspects within the self-assessment. This emphasizes the importance of having a single self-assessment writer to pull things together.

Assessors don't expect your provision to be perfect; they expect to see descriptions of weaknesses as well as strengths. In the former case, make sure to include your plans for correcting the weaknesses, and in the latter, outline the mechanisms by which good practice is disseminated. Do this over a specific time frame, for instance change and development in the previous two to three years.

Collect a sample of self-assessments from your own institution and from colleagues in other institutions. (You might find a few on the Web, but you have to know where to find them!) While they are all specific to the aims and objectives of the providers concerned, they might give you some good ideas.

How are self-assessments analysed?

The entire description and evaluation of provision is based on the aims and objectives, so this should be the first thing that the assessors look at. HEFCE will ask if they are clear enough to be published in the quality assessment report and if they form an adequate basis on which to construct an agenda for the assessment visit. The *Assessors' Handbook* (HEFCE, 1996a) suggests the following questions for assessing the clarity of the aims and objectives.

- Do the aims express the broad purposes for each programme in the subject?
- Do the aims state the abilities and aptitudes that can be expected of the successful graduate?
- Do the objectives define the intentions for the student learning experience and learning outcomes for each programme?
- Are the aims and objectives clear enough to form a framework for the assessment?
- Are the aims and objectives consistent with the institutional mission, where applicable?
- Is there a clear relationship between the stated aims and objectives?

Writing the subject aims and objectives can be difficult and these questions should be considered carefully. That providers have frequently violated one requirement or another is repeatedly noted in the subject overview reports published to date, although statements of aims and objectives are gradually improving.

The reporting assessor normally analyses the evaluation section of the self-assessment, using the assessors' *aide-mémoire* (HEFCE, 1996a) prior to the preparatory meeting for the visit, at which he or she may seek further clarification. The *aide-mémoire* asks, for each aspect, what is stated in the self-assessment in relation to the aspect, and what specific objectives are relevant to the aspect. Again, this encourages close scrutiny of the aims and objectives.

When analysing a self-assessment document assessors will also focus on any assertion, apparent complacency or anything that might seem unusual or out of context for the subject. Summarized below is a useful set of questions suggested for analysing self-assessments in *Making the Grade* (UCoSDA and Loughborough University, 1996).

- Are the aims and objectives clearly stated?
- Are the aims achievable, given the stated objectives, the available resources and the student profile?
- Have curricula been designed to achieve the aims and objectives, including appropriate specific and transferable skills?
- Are students informed of the curricular content?
- Are the teaching methods described?
- Is the range of opportunities for student learning described?
- Does assessment promote learning as well as judge progress?
- Is student progression and achievement clearly documented and satisfactory?
- Do graduates gain relevant employment or progress to further study?
- Do students receive effective academic and pastoral support?
- Are the learning resources, including staff expertise, appropriate to the achievement of the aims and objectives?
- Do staff participate in professional development activities? What is the impact of staff research and scholarship on the provision?
- Are the quality assurance and enhancement mechanisms effective?
- Are the views of students sought and acted on?
- Are the views of external sources, such as examiners and employers, taken into account?

You should be able to answer these questions in the case of your own completed self-assessment. Another handy checklist is the section on characteristics of the education assessed, in the HEFCE *Report on Quality Assessment 1995–96* (HEFCE, 1997b).

Writing the Framework – subject aims and objectives

The institutional mission

You might start with a statement of the institutional mission. Only do this if you can clearly demonstrate the link between the mission and your aims and objectives at subject level. For example, if your institution prides itself on its commitment to widening access, is this supported by the *subject* access policy and statistics? The subject overview reports for subjects assessed in the 1995–96 round note that many providers do include the institutional mission, and describe how the subject aims complement it. However, while assessors may be interested in links to the institutional mission, their primary concern is the statement of the subject-level aims and objectives.

Programmes under assessment

Here you list all the programmes that come under the subject being assessed. For many providers it may be just one or two programmes, for others it can be a very wide range. In the case of monotechnic institutions, such as Dartington College of Arts, the list of programmes might include the entire institutional provision.

One problem for subject providers with a large number of programmes is the specification of the aims and objectives for separate programmes. The best approach here is to specify a core set of aims and objectives appropriate to all programmes, such as enabling students to pursue independent study of the subject, and then append short lists specific to each programme.

We emphasize that objectives must be stated for each taught programme under assessment. The subject overview reports show that many providers neglect to specify particular aims and objectives for postgraduate programmes. This might be because they view postgraduate programmes as simply an advanced extension of undergraduate programmes. However, many postgraduate programmes are 'conversion courses' inducting graduates from other fields into the subject, and such an aim should be explicitly stated.

Aims and objectives

Considering the importance of aims and objectives there is surprisingly little guidance on writing them. Terms such as 'aims', 'objectives', 'goals', 'mission', 'learning outcomes' are highly ambiguous at the best of times and HEFCE has chosen not to be prescriptive on this. For HEFCE, 'aims' represent your 'broad purposes' in relation to the subject; 'objectives' relate to specific programmes and are usually given in two forms: the intended student learning experiences (process) and what the student will be able to do on completion of the programme (outcomes).

HEFCE subject aims

The definition of the aims of a programme under HEFCE quality assessment is given in HEFCE Circular 39/94.

> 'The aims express the subject provider's broad purposes in presenting each programme of study in the subject.'

HEFCE advises you to express your aims for a programme in terms of the sorts of abilities and attitudes the stakeholders in higher education can expect of a student who successfully completes the programme. It recognizes that different institutions may have different aims but suggests some typical ways in which they might be expressed:

- 'the meeting of local, regional or national needs;
- preparation for research;
- preparation for the world of work, including satisfaction of professional body requirements;
- social goals, such as widening access or increasing the degree of student choice and control over study pattern;
- enabling students to pursue independent study in the subject.' (HEFCE, 1994c)

For modular, multi-subject or interdisciplinary schemes, you will need to clarify the contribution of the subject to the aims of the overall scheme.

A perusal of the aims quoted in quality assessment reports soon reveals that many providers have taken to heart the above examples of expressing aims. Assessors have pointed to the widespread use of 'somewhat formulaic phrases related to highest standards in teaching, scholarship and research, and enabling students to realize their full potential' (HEFCE, 1996e). Specific subject aims are often quite similar across providers in a given subject; for example, a large proportion of providers have aims relating to generic or transferable skills. Some providers have quite distinctive aims; for example, some providers in chemical engineering have the laudable aim of inculcating environmental and social awareness. A significant proportion of providers do not distinguish clearly between aims and objectives and also fail to show clear links between them.

HEFCE subject objectives

The definition of the objectives of a programme under HEFCE quality assessment is given in Circular 39/94:

'The objectives set out the intended student learning experiences and student achievements that demonstrate successful completion of a programme of study.' (HEFCE, 1994c)

Note that these are the *subject provider's* objectives. The intended experiences and achievements to which they relate may be expressed in terms of the expected learning outcomes of the academic programme, examples of which include:

- the acquisition of knowledge;
- the development of understanding and other general intellectual abilities;
- the development of conceptual, intellectual and subject-specific skills;
- the development of generic or transferable skills;
- the development of values, of motivation or attitudes to learning.

Apart from the 500 word limit for aims and objectives, the self-assessment writer has little to go on. For quality assessments conducted after April 1995 the subject aims and objectives are published verbatim in the quality assessment reports. This provides 272 examples of sets of subject aims and objectives. Published reports are available on the Web (http://www. niss.ac.uk/education/hefce/qar/).

There is a wide variation in styles of presentation of aims and objectives, probably reflecting the lack of guidance in writing them. On the other hand, the examples given by HEFCE occur frequently. Some sets of aims and objectives are short and succinct, others verbose and rambling. Some contain irrelevant information, such as the outcomes of the RAE, and others omit what are obvious features of the provision. In the post-April 1995 methodology the subject overview reports discuss the aims and objectives of providers in each subject, and they are a rich source of ideas.

The link between aims and objectives

It is important to realize that the objectives must be related to the aims; in fact, the basis on which assessors' judgements are reached is 'meeting the objectives set by the subject provider, and the extent to which the objectives set, and the level of attainment of those objectives, allow the aims set by the subject provider to be met' (HEFCE, 1995b). As mentioned above, not all providers make this link transparent, listing aims and objectives that are virtually independent or bear little relation to each other. However, a good example of specific links between aims and objectives is provided by those of French at Oxford Brookes University (HEFCE, 1996d). This is also a good example of dealing with the aims and objectives of a range of programmes. Very briefly, there are four programmes forming the basis of the assessment:

> BA (Joint Honours) French Language and Contemporary Studies (FS)
> BA (Joint Honours) French Language and Literature (FL)
> BA (Single Honours/double field) Languages for Business (LB)
> MA Culture and Society in Modern France and/or Germany (MA).

Nine aims are expressed for all programmes, of which five are common and the rest are specific to each programme. For example, the first two aims stated are:

> 'The academic programme delivered by LB, FL, FS and the MA provides the opportunity for students to prepare, through growth of knowledge and personal development, for life beyond the University, enabling students to:
> *i*   develop a command of spoken and written French appropriate to effective communication in academic, social and practical situations

   ii (a) (LB) develop awareness of the business environment in France
       (b) (FL) understand, through the study of French Literature, the nature and value of literary creation and the literary product
       (c) (FS) understand the social and political structures of contemporary France
       (d) (MA) explore higher level areas of intellectual interest relating to France.'

Here *i* is an aim common to all programmes, while *ii* specifies a separate aim for each programme. For each aim, related objectives are then specified. For example, the objectives for the aim *i* above are:

'Students will develop strategies for systematic language study, acquisition and practice leading to a high level of competence in all four language skills. They will:

  (a) *Aural, oral skills*
- achieve competence in the use of spoken French as the language of instruction and learning
- communicate effectively with educated native speakers in academic, social and practical situations
- achieve expertise in oral presentation and argumentation.

  (b) *Reading skills*
develop lexical and discourse skills to support intensive and extensive reading of a wide range of non-specialist and semi-specialist texts in contemporary French and of literary texts.

  (c) *Writing skills*
learn to use accurately the grammar and syntax of written French and deploy a range of discourse conventions, models and structures in argumentation, narrative and descriptive writing to produce written texts for academic, imaginative, practical and institutional purposes.'

In this example the objectives are expressed in terms of clear learning outcomes and are clearly linked to the aims. The aims of different programmes are itemized in a distinct manner.

For a specific example of a breakdown in the link between aims and objectives picked up by assessors note the following quote from an assessment of English:

'Although almost all English providers include preparation for employment in their aims and objectives, in practice such aims are seldom articulated in the form of specific learning objectives.' (HEFCE, 1995g)

Terminology on objectives and outcomes

After much debate and soul searching we have decided to come clean on our (lack of) understanding of HEFCE terminology on such things as 'objectives' and 'learning outcomes'. We *think* we have it sorted out (assuming that it can be sorted out). The problem is that in all the HEFCE quality assessment literature, ancient and modern, such terms are used variously and, dare we say it, vaguely. In the HEFCE circulars describing the quality assessment methodology and procedures, there is something approaching consistency, but in such things as quality assessment reports, anarchy reigns.

References to objectives and outcomes are made in the framework to the self-assessment, in the *aide-mémoire*, the teaching observation proforma and the student work proforma in the *Assessors' Handbook*. It is the usage in the *Assessors' Handbook* that is most confusing where we find 'subject objectives', 'specific objectives', 'learning objectives', 'session objectives', 'intended learning outcomes' and 'intended outcomes of teaching and learning'. Unfortunately, the context does not always remove the ambiguity.

The confusion is compounded by the fact that terms such as 'learning objectives' and 'learning outcomes' can have a technical meaning in some educational literature. HEFCE does not use any accepted technical definitions; the only definitions it gives are of aims and objectives at *subject* level, in terms of the *expected learning outcomes* of the academic programme. As we noted earlier, these are implicitly defined in terms of 'acquisition of knowledge, development of understanding and other general intellectual abilities, the development of conceptual, intellectual and subject specific skills, the development of generic and transferable skills, or the development of values, of motivation or attitudes to learning' (HEFCE, 1995b).

'Specific objectives' used in the assessors' *aide-mémoire* refers to particular subject objectives that relate to and have an impact on a given aspect. Under the TLA aspect these are called 'learning objectives', ie they are the specific subject objectives having an impact on the TLA aspect. They can be expressed as intended learning outcomes of the sort noted above; that is, the intended learning outcomes are simply the learning objectives.

HEFCE does not explicitly refer to objectives at the course or module level. In the *aide-mémoire* for the CDCO aspect they refer to 'intended outcomes of teaching and learning' and *these* may be at any level: programme, course, or session.

The only other objectives referred to are the 'session objectives' in the teaching observation form (Annex E, *Assessors' Handbook*). These are the objectives of the observed teaching session, which of course will be related to one or more of the learning objectives.

Our interpretation of the HEFCE terminology, which we use throughout the rest of this book, is summarized as follows:

- 'Aims' will only be used at the subject/programme level.
- 'Objectives' may be defined at subject/programme, course/module, and teaching session level, when we use, respectively:
  - subject objectives
  - course objectives
  - session objectives.

This defines a *hierarchy of objectives*. There should be clear links between each level of this hierarchy.

- 'Learning objectives' are the specific subject objectives for the TLA aspect, ie all subject objectives relating to student learning. Strictly speaking, learning objectives may be defined at all levels, but HEFCE only uses the term at subject level.
- 'Intended outcome' is a synonym for an objective and may be used at any level, ie an 'intended learning outcome' is a learning objective.

Key properties of subject providers' objectives

As mentioned earlier, the subject overview reports comment on the nature and quality of providers' aims and objectives. We can glean useful guidelines from such comments. Broadly, we can say that well-written subject objectives should be:

- focused (eg vocational) with a sense of purpose;
- complete in that they encompass all aspects of the provision and do not omit anything significant;
- appropriately located in the hierarchy from institutional mission down to individual teaching session;
- achievable;
- at an appropriate standard;
- measurable by internal mechanisms to the satisfaction of the assessors;
- effectively communicated to all stakeholders.

It is worth summarizing some of the specific comments about aims and objectives arising from the 1995–96 round of assessments, reported in the subject overview reports. The key points raised relate to:

- clarity of aims and objectives;
- the lack of distinction between aims and objectives;
- lack of reference to aims and objectives in the body of the self-assessment;
- variation in the 'ambition' of aims;
- not reporting aims for different programmes, particularly for taught postgraduate programmes;
- lack of indication of how specific objectives will be achieved, particularly those relating to generic or transferable skills;
- variations in the specificity of objectives;
- subject aims and objectives relatively poor for modular programmes – lack of coherence.

Formulating aims and objectives for the self-assessment

For some subject providers the self-assessment is the first time that they articulate their subject aims and objectives. Usually, it is at the course level that
'objectives' are specified, for example in a student handbook. Subject-level
intentions are often implicit in the portfolio of programmes offered, or they
may be tucked away in the departmental academic plan. Even so, it is
unlikely that they will be expressed in the precise form required for the self-
assessment. So, how do we formulate these subject-level aims and objectives?
Aims are often already implicit in current documentation such as prospectuses, programme descriptions and academic plans. By linking them to the
institutional mission, this can provide an overall direction for the subject
provider aims. Anyone reading the aims should get a good idea of why the
programmes are being run and why at that institution.

One way to formulate subject objectives is to start with a clean slate and
canvass a wide range of views, for instance from students, staff and employers. Take a look at examples of aims and objectives in related subjects. A
brainstorming session with all staff involved in the assessment can result in
a set of objectives expressing what it is that you intend as a provider, and also
ensure ownership of the outcome. Once you have a rough starting point for
the objectives, refine them by checking the key properties referred to above:
that they cover all your provision; are measurable and achievable; they are
set at the right standard (broadly commensurate with level of study); they
link subject aims to course and 'lower objectives'; and they are documented
and communicated to staff and students.

There are no guidelines on the number of objectives, but as only 500 words
are allowed for the framework, there are clear limits. Often the resulting
objectives may be grouped, for example, into 'general educational', 'curriculum' and 'personal/transferable'. The list may represent 'the ideal', so it must
be checked that the provision actually measures up! A classic example here
is the frequently chosen objective of 'encouraging independent learning
skills'. If you say you do it, assessors look for evidence that you do – and on
many occasions they have found this not to be the case. If you do develop
such skills you might describe how you do this under the TLA, SSG and LR
aspects, ie how it fits into the programme of teaching and learning activities,
how it is supported and how it is resourced.

An alternative approach to obtaining the subject objectives is to look at
what the current programmes do or contain and construct your list of aims
and objectives from those of the courses/modules in the programmes. This
assumes that your aims and objectives are manifested in your portfolio of
programmes – they are implicit in what you already do.

Students, staff and learning resources

This section is largely about data gathering – obtaining the statistics on the student profile, the details relating to staff (don't forget part-time or visiting staff) and the learning resources available. If you have good management information statistics, this section should present few difficulties.

Evaluation of the quality of education

This part of the self-assessment has to be succinct; it allows just 4,000 words to describe your entire provision *and* provide or signpost evidence to support your evaluation of its quality. What should you include? Have you missed anything important? How much description and in what detail? How much evaluation? What sort of evidence goes in? What can be left until the visit? Importantly, this section of the self-assessment must relate to the subject aims and objectives at all times. It must convince the reader that there is the possibility that aims and objectives could be achieved. The evidence, included or signposted, must confirm that the described provision does achieve the aims and objectives.

Always ensure that your objectives are backed up by statistical information whenever possible; for example if one objective is to prepare students for research in the field, it should be possible to demonstrate the proportion of students who go on to research and who succeed in research. If an objective is to prepare students for a particular career, employment data should confirm this. If you have a diverse student profile, such as ethnic mix, part-time/full-time, overseas, European, non-standard qualifications, make sure that you have good cohort statistics to reflect this (assessors have found weaknesses here). Claims made about such things as good employment record of graduates need to be considered in relation to *national* statistics in your subject, not just your own figures. This is a general principle of evidence: your local statistics need to be compared to national statistics in the subject.

Evidence to support the evaluation of the provision may be assembled using the issues/evidence grids described in Chapter 2 (pages 30–31). The evidence for a particular part of the provision will come from a selection (at least two) of the sources matched against that provision on the grid. For each source of evidence in the grid you can fill in a measure of the quality under that item, the information provided by that source, a measure of its validity and reliability and its location (self-assessment, base room, other). This may seem like a large task, but it should not be done grudgingly. The systematic rigour should pay dividends in opportunities for development and should itself provide an impressive quality assurance tool for the QAE aspect. So, it is now a matter of working systematically through the key issues for each aspect of provision. We do this in detail in Chapters 4–9.

The annexes

The four optional annexes are described at the beginning of this chapter. The statistical indicators do not necessarily measure performance or quality but provide background and context. Summary tables on the courses offered, students enrolled, completion rates and achievement are especially helpful to the assessors in understanding the context of the subject within the institution. The more information that can be summarized in the annexes, the more space is available in the main body of the self-assessment to describe and evaluate the provision. Statistical indicators may also provide evidence for the Evaluation of the Quality of Education section of the self-assessment.

Chapter 4

Curriculum design, content and organization

This chapter covers issues for curriculum design, content and organization (CDCO).

1. Structure and content of curricula

Consistency of curricula with the subject aims and objectives in terms of:
(a) special characteristics of the provision, including recognition of professional/ accrediting bodies
(b) breadth, depth and coherence
(c) student profile, progression and achievement
(d) flexibility and student choice
(e) specialisms of academic staff.

2. Intended outcomes of the curricula

(f) clearly defined and communicated intended outcomes of teaching and learning
(g) consistency of learning opportunities with the subject aims and objectives in terms of:
 – subject-specific and generic/transferable skills
 – vocational competencies and progression to employment
 – progression to further study
 – personal development.

3. Currency and innovative features

(h) curricula informed by recent developments in the subject and in teaching and learning
(i) curricula informed by professional activities of staff.

Introduction

The CDCO aspect essentially covers the 'what' of the educational provision: the content of your programmes, how it is organized, the intended learning outcomes and the currency of the programmes. Currently, under the HEFCE system, your aims and objectives are not questioned, but assessors expect the curriculum content and its organization to ensure that they are achievable. For example, if one of the subject objectives is to produce economists with an understanding of business practices, assessors would probably expect to see courses in business studies. If such courses were only optional, then some students might be able to complete the programme without meeting that objective and assessors would draw attention to this.

What the assessors say on the CDCO aspect

Overall, there appears to be considerable satisfaction with the CDCO aspect of provision across HEFCE institutions. Roughly two-thirds of providers in the 1995–96 round achieved a grade 3 for this aspect and only 7 per cent a grade 2. This may be because it is the area in which there has traditionally been a considerable amount of quality assurance. Well-established systems already exist for designing, validating and monitoring programme content and organization through internal committees, professional accreditation and external examiners. There are many subject experts around to provide peer review and to keep programmes up to date. Yet some reservations remain; interestingly, it is often the provision of generic or transferable skills which attracts comment in this aspect.

Things that assessors have commented favourably on and which form the characteristics of high quality provision under this aspect include:

- well designed broad and coherent curricula matched to aims and objectives;
- good academic progression between years/modules with appropriate intellectual challenge;
- good match between staff expertise and the curriculum;
- effective links with employers, industry, commerce, the professions, PSBs and subject associations;
- beneficial impact of staff scholarship (and research where present in the aims and objectives) on the curriculum;
- effective integration and assessment of subject knowledge, subject skills and generic skills;
- modular programmes with coherent pathways, structures, and academic progression. Student guidance on choices and combinations;

- students' contribution to the design and management of the curriculum; choice and flexibility for students within clear and well understood structures;
- effective exploitation of modern technology;
- clear differentiation of the programmes for undergraduate and postgraduate students. (HEFCE, 1997b)

On the negative side, assessors found that the aims and objectives of some providers were not being fully achieved. For example, under business studies (pre-April 1995 assessment round) about 40 per cent of institutions that have the aim of developing the students' knowledge and skills in a European or international business context did not achieve this. For modern languages, assessors drew attention to the fact that the period abroad is not always effectively integrated into the curriculum. This issue of integration and coherence of the programme was echoed in regard to generic or transferable skills.

Sources of evidence for the CDCO aspect

The sources of evidence are largely paper-based. Assessors scrutinize departmental literature that describes your provision to students, including: student prospectus and handbook, accreditation documentation and external examiners' reports. If these are provided over a range of years, it will give a picture of how the curriculum has changed or adapted. In particular, internal validation and review documentation may provide useful evidence about currency and innovations and the effectiveness of quality assurance and enhancement mechanisms. Assessors speak to employers and graduates during the visit, which gives them valuable feedback on the currency and relevance of the curriculum. They will also draw conclusions based on their own subject expertise, experience and the observation of teaching sessions.

Be alert to conflicting terminology between assessment and accreditation documentation, particularly terms such as 'course', 'module' and 'learning outcomes'. If it is some time since accreditation, assessors may want to know whether you have kept your curriculum up to date to meet the evolving accreditation needs, and what you are doing to prepare for the next accreditation visit.

If accreditation is refused, or only given for a shorter period than normal, this will not necessarily affect the quality assessment outcome. The accrediting body may have different priorities in relation to the curricula. If possible, the documentation and other requirements of accreditation, quality assessment and internal mechanisms should be harmonized to avoid duplication of effort. For example, accrediting bodies often ask for curricula to be described in a format different to that used internally, leaving assessors with the unenviable task of matching the two together. Provide good clear documentation on this for assessors – do the matching for them.

The key issues for this aspect are set out at the beginning of the chapter, and are explored in more detail below.

1. Structure and content of curricula

The issues here relate to how, for each level and mode of study, the structure and content of the curricula match up to the subject aims and objectives in terms of any special features, breadth, depth and coherence, student profile and progression, flexibility and choice, and the expertise of staff.

Level and mode of study

The curricula need to be described for each level of programme, ie at undergraduate, diploma and postgraduate level. Assessors have noticed a tendency for providers to be less diligent in the description and evaluation of taught postgraduate provision.

For most providers the mode of study is fairly conventional, usually full-time study on-campus. With the exception of the Open University, most higher education students take a full-time three-year degree. Some take a four-year thick or thin sandwich course and some attend part time. There are, however, an increasing number of distance learning programmes and, with the growing emphasis on lifelong learning and CATS, the mode of study is likely to become more varied. This will have implications for the structure and content of curricula. The Open University provides a good example, where specially developed foundation courses are available to accommodate the wide variety of backgrounds and abilities of the students. The Open University curricula are also spelt out very carefully, usually with detailed course objectives, so that students are clear about what is expected of them and can make informed choices.

Consistency of objectives and the curricula

A major issue under the CDCO aspect is the relationship between the curricula provided and the stated subject aims and objectives. For subject-specific objectives such as 'students will be able to use Italian to a high level of accuracy and fluency in a wide variety of academic and social situations', it is fairly straightforward to construct a curriculum that delivers this. Providers may find more difficulty in designing curricula to meet generic and transferable skills, however. In such cases the content and structure of the curricula required may be less familiar to the subject specialist and demand a wider range of learning opportunities. A good example of developing students' communication skills is given in the quality assessment report for chemical engineering at Loughborough (HEFCE, 1995d):

> 'Students' communication skills are developed effectively through the use of the University's excellent flexible learning materials; there are requirements for oral presentations, with feedback provided from peer and staff comment and playback of video recordings. The flexible learning materials include a first-year exercise in report writing, which was developed in collaboration with the Department's staff.'

This example includes a wide range of learning opportunities, requiring the students to engage in a number of activities to develop all aspects of their communication skills.

Assessors have identified conflict between the curricula and the aims and objectives. Examples include failure to translate certain objectives into specific curricula content and structure; narrow curricula conflicting with objectives for a wide, or broad provision; weaknesses in linking industrial training or a period abroad to objectives; and the lack of opportunities for independent learning. It is important to emphasize that assessors are not seeking to prescribe what you teach, merely to assess the extent to which the opportunities you do provide enable your objectives to be achieved.

The best means of clarifying the link between the curricula and the subject aims and objectives is to ensure that programme and course content is clearly defined by specifying precise course objectives or learning outcomes. There is substantial literature on this topic, but essentially a good educational objective is one which contains an *action verb* describing an *observable* and *measurable* performance, along with statements of the *conditions* imposed on the performance and the *standards* to be reached (Gronlund, 1978; Mager, 1990). Alternative descriptors of educational intent include *learning outcomes* and *competency descriptors*, but they all boil down to Mager's original definition of an educational objective. Fundamentally, you must have some means of specifying precisely what you intend the student to be able to do on completion of a particular course, under what conditions and to what standard.

(a) Special characteristics of the provision

Your provision may have characteristics that make the curriculum unique or distinctive. It may be an emphasis on a particular part of the subject, for example polymer chemistry and plastics in a chemical engineering programme, or a focus on local issues or industrial applications. Whatever the specialism, the aims and objectives should reflect it and assessors should be able to see support for these in your curriculum. Students may have been attracted to your programme by such distinctive features; assessors may ask them if the programme lived up to its promise in this respect.

If one of your aims relates to meeting the requirements of a professional accrediting body, this should be reflected in the curricula. Accreditation is essential in some subjects, particularly in engineering, in order to attract students. The accrediting body might set tight requirements on the curriculum and there will certainly be a basic core of material that will be essential, but that still leaves room for distinctive features and specialisms.

(b) Breadth, depth and coherence

Aim for the balance between breadth and depth implied in your aims and objectives. Don't confuse depth with 'theoretical underpinning'; it refers to the level of detail that you go into. Experimental topics can be just as deep as theoretical ones. Don't confuse breadth with 'surface learning'; breadth refers to the range of topics covered. Assessors have noted particular difficulties with breadth and depth in modular programmes.

The things that assessors might pick up under this issue include lack of depth, too much superficial study, or excessive depth inappropriate to the subject. An example of the last would be detailed pure mathematics courses used as service courses for engineers. Assessors could also notice an inappropriate balance of depth and breadth, producing students who are not 'well rounded'. In teaching observation they may see staff following their own interests at the expense of a balanced curriculum.

You can avoid such problems by maximizing staff and external input to curriculum design, so that a wide range of perspectives is brought to bear. Seek the views of outsiders such as external examiners and employers. You can give indications of intended depth and breadth by specifying precise course objectives or learning outcomes.

Programmes should be coherent in that courses fit together in logical, structured sequences. The lack of coherence and structure is often commented on by assessors; in particular modularized courses have come in for considerable criticism in this respect (and, in fact, many other respects). Student choice needs to be well supported in order to achieve coherence in modularized programmes. Sometimes, modules overlap in content, with the result that students study the same material twice.

Assessors may look at departmental literature, to check that prerequisites and co-requisites are clearly indicated. They may ask students if they experience difficulties in the transition between courses. In teaching observation they will be able to see if staff are clear about how their courses fit into the overall programme. Assessors may pick up on the lack of exchange of ideas between courses, poorly designed prerequisites and co-requisites, the fragmented view of the subject, and the lack of communication between staff.

These problems can be avoided by careful programme design with approp-riate chaining and sequencing. Make sure different study pathways are well defined and explained, perhaps in a student handbook.

Related to coherence is the degree of integration of specialist courses into the curriculum. For example, you might provide a single one-off course in information technology to develop the students' IT skills. This is not as effec-tive as integrating such training into the curriculum, providing opportunities for its development in the core subjects, in addition to providing bespoke IT courses. Lack of coordination between practical subjects and their theoretical underpinning can also undermine the coherence of a programme, as can the lack of integration of serviced units. The availability of optional courses can affect the coherence if it permits students to avoid fundamental areas of the subject.

Useful references on programme and course design, which address some of the issues raised above, include Rowntree (1981, 1982), Ellington *et al.* (1993), Jenkins and Walker (1994), Baume and Baume (1992).

(c) Student profile, progression and achievement

The intended student profile will be clear from your entry requirements and access arrangements. The profile has implications for the curriculum. A parti-cularly thorny problem here is the design of the first-year curricula to accom-modate changes in pre-university curricula and to provide a smooth transition to higher education in the face of an increasingly diverse student profile. This is particularly problematic in the case of degree programmes relying on serial subjects such as mathematics, physics, English, languages and history. Assessment of some engineering programmes and modern lan-guages has already drawn attention to this problem. Responses include remedial tuition, bridging courses and foundation years.

Since it is very difficult to predict students' abilities from their entry qual-ifications, some form of initial assessment must be built into the curriculum. A common mistake, often noted by assessors, is to pile this 'remedial' mate-rial into the first-year curriculum without taking anything out. All this achieves is an increased workload on already hard-pressed students, simply compounding their problems, which is particularly acute in the case of non-standard entry qualifications. The issue is linked to the TLA and SSG aspects, ie how such students are taught and supported.

Many institutions are now taking *ab initio* students into their language pro-grammes, raising the question of how these are phased into the programme with fellow students who have previous experience of the language. Not sur-prisingly, assessors have noted problems with this in some provision, mainly relating to the excessive workload imposed on *ab initio* students. The design of the first-year curriculum therefore requires careful thought, allowing for the heterogeneous student profile and shifting material into subsequent years with consequent knock-on effects.

Equally, allowance for overseas students will become increasingly important as overseas recruitment increases. Such students bring with them their own specific needs, not the least being language support. Assessors may want to know how these are dealt with in the curriculum. Are there courses in English as a second language for such students and are they integrated into the curriculum? Again, if you have a high proportion of mature students, or students from a professional background, does the curriculum support them, or even build on their strengths?

Does the curriculum structure enable students to progress easily from one stage of a programme to the next? For example, if student weaknesses in the first year necessitate pushing material into the second year, this may have a knock-on effect in the final year, making it difficult to achieve the programme objectives. Or you may push students very hard in the first year in order to 'catch-up', resulting in high failure rates and low achievement, which distorts the progression statistics. Under the SPA aspect assessors will look at the progression and achievement statistics and if they notice any anomalies they will search for a cause. Will they find this in the structure and content of your curriculum?

(d) Flexibility and student choice

Flexibility in curriculum provision refers to the degree of student choice, the number of options/modules, the ease of transfer between them and the range of qualifications and progression routes available. It also relates to access policies and possible study pathway options offered and is particularly relevant to modularized courses. Flexibility must be supported by opportunities for smooth transition between chosen pathways. Are there opportunities for students to transfer between courses at different levels to enable them to adjust their educational programme to their abilities and experience? Is there a good balance between specialization and individual development? For example, assessors have come across modular programmes in which students are expected to choose pathways for themselves with little guidance.

Other problems include students taking little advantage of flexibility and choice, most following one or two popular pathways; timetabling difficulties; conflict between choice and coherence; poor documentation and support on choice; implicit unintentional biases on choices if, for example, some options are easier than others; and clustering of workload. Resolving such problems calls for careful organization of the curriculum. Key areas in need of particular attention are timetables matched to study pathways; uniform standards across offerings; support and guidance for students on pathway choices; and clearly articulated educational objectives in modular schemes and courses generally.

(e) Specialisms of academic staff

Clearly, you must have the appropriate complement of staff to deliver the curriculum. In these days of stretched resources it is not always possible to match staff expertise to the curriculum and assessors will appreciate this. They are likely to have similar problems in their own institutions. In fact, it would appear that HEFCE also has difficulty finding staff with the right specialisms to conduct assessments (HEFCE, 1997b). Many institutions now place considerable reliance on part-time staff and in this case you should outline how such staff are supported and integrated into the provision. Assessors have picked up examples where achievement of the objectives was frustrated by too few, or inappropriately qualified, staff. For providers in German and related languages serious deficiencies in staffing have been penalized with a grade 1 in the LR aspect.

Assessors will be able to get some idea of the staff specialisms from the self-assessment which they can then compare with the prospectus and syllabuses. However, the teaching observation will be the most telling; from teaching observation assessors will be able to form a good picture of the match between curricula and expertise. Assessors will probably recognize when staff lack subject expertise, do not keep up to date, or do not appreciate the context of their material. When expertise is lost by staff departures, you must either ensure that it is replaced, or change the curriculum to match the expertise available. This may also mean changing the subject aims and objectives. Make sure that new staff are assigned appropriately to courses within their expertise, are given adequate preparation time, and have training in course design and development.

2. Intended outcomes of the curricula

(f) Clearly defined and communicated intended outcomes of teaching and learning

Here we are referring to the intended outcomes of any teaching and learning activities, in any part of the curricula and at any level, ie programme, course or individual teaching session. Essentially, the objectives of any learning activity should be clear and documented. The subject aims and objectives convey the intended learning outcomes at the subject level. The intended learning outcomes of the courses within the programme(s) must also be documented. Many providers now do this in a student handbook. It is less usual to specify precise objectives for individual sessions (corresponding to the schoolteachers' lesson plan) but this can certainly be done for the classes observed during the visit.

There might be many other forms of learning activities, such as project work or field work. Again, the intended learning outcomes of such activities should be clearly defined and documented, so that the students know exactly what the activity is intended to achieve. A good rule of thumb is that an assessor should be able to find a documented statement of the objectives of any learning activity that he or she comes across. These issues are explored further in Chapter 5 where we consider teaching, learning and assessment strategies.

(g) Consistency of learning opportunities with subject aims and objectives

Subject-specific and transferable skills

This issue relates to the type of learning experience on offer to the student. There should be a range of learning opportunities such as lectures, tutorials, practicals, coursework and independent learning, as appropriate to the aims and objectives. A clear understanding of the link between the teaching, learning and assessment strategy and the learning objectives is required (see Chapter 5). The assessors can gain some evidence on this from the departmental literature, but most will come from teaching observation.

Sometimes the learning opportunities are not appropriate to the learning objectives. Some provision, such as lectures, may be too passive to *be* learning opportunities. For example, counselling skills cannot be taught by simply lecturing to the students – role play exercises would be much more appropriate. Another possible weakness is the provision of poor learning materials for independent learning. There are two issues here: whether a particular learning opportunity is appropriate to the learning objective, and whether the opportunity is actually delivered effectively.

An area that has attracted considerable comment from the assessors is that of generic or transferable skills. Examples of such skills are listed on page 64 (Gibbs *et al.*, 1994).

Transferable skills	Examples
Communication	Report writing, presentation skills
Group work	Leadership, chairing meetings, cooperation, teamwork
Personal	Independence and autonomy, self-assessment, self-reliance
Interpersonal	Influencing, counselling, interviewing, negotiation
Organizational	Time and project management, objective-setting
Teaching and training	Identifying learning needs, designing and running workshops, coaching, peer tutoring
Learning	Reading and note-taking with purpose, literature search and review
Information gathering	Locating information sources, evaluating sources and data, extracting relevant information, interpretation of data
Problem solving	Problem analysis, creative problem solving, decision making
Language	Oral skills, use of a foreign language
Information technology	Word-processing, databases, spreadsheets, graphics, desktop publishing
Entrepreneurship	Taking initiatives and opportunities, creativity

Such skills may be developed within the subject-specific areas in the process of learning other subjects, through specially dedicated courses, or by industrial placements or periods abroad.

The failure to integrate transferable skills into the curriculum is a common criticism from assessors. Similarly, objectives relating to transferable skills are not always translated into appropriate learning opportunities. Training, or lack of it, in IT skills has come in for particular criticism across a range of subjects, occurring frequently in assessors' recommendations. Another common criticism voiced by assessors concerns the lack of assessment of transferable skills that providers claim to develop.

In contrast, assessors have also come across many imaginative ways in which transferable skills are integrated into a subject. These include the planning of conferences and meetings by students under the direction of staff; role play and management games; design and building of team exercises; international exchange visits.

Vocational competencies

Assessors are generally complimentary about opportunities offered for vocational competencies and providers tend to do well in this area. This is probably because most vocational subjects, such as pharmacy or electrical engineering, have significant professional input, or are accredited by a professional body. Ensure that the required vocational competencies are understood and documented. Assessors may ask graduates about the relevance of the curriculum to their careers or further study and, where relevant, about the sorts of opportunities for practical and vocational experience provided by their programme. You can ensure that your education in vocational competencies is up to date through good liaison with employers or feedback from industrial placements. Assessors can also talk to employers or review feedback from them.

Further study

If one of your objectives is the progression to further study, you need to be specific about this and be able to explain how your provision accommodates it. Cohort statistics should also back up your claims. Assessors will ask if your programme provides an appropriate starting point for continuing study of the subject – does it provide an appropriate foundation of breadth and depth at the appropriate level? Your programme details will give the assessors some idea and they will get more information from teaching observation and talking to staff and students.

Personal development

The HEQC *Graduate Standards Programme* (HEQC, 1996a) has proposed a list of qualities to be expected in graduates, including their ability to undertake their own personal development. Under personal development, HEQC includes self-reflection, self-criticism, intellectual maturity and judgement, autonomy, appreciation of values, response to change, questioning received wisdom and the ability to instigate change as needed. Designing learning opportunities that encourage the acquisition of such skills is not easy and it is doubtful whether assessors over-exert themselves in seeking them out. But it is easy to argue that the total experience of three or more years of intensive study, coupled with wide-ranging social and professional interactions should provide plenty of scope for personal development.

As far as the curriculum is concerned, such learning opportunities as project work, industrial placements and a period abroad can also contribute towards students' personal development. In fact, few providers actually have an objective in the area of personal development. However, German at Leeds University was commended for its use of a personal skills portfolio during students' first-year and a year-abroad experience log.

3. Currency and innovative features

(h) Curricula informed by recent developments in the subject and in teaching and learning

Most providers are good at keeping up to date on the developments in their subject – it is one of the reasons that research and scholarship are so important in higher education institutions. Long-established systems for programme review exist in most institutions, and input from external examiners, professional bodies and employers keep departments on their toes. However, it does no harm to impress assessors with proactive means of keeping informed about subject developments by, for example, encouraging staff to publish in educational journals devoted to their subject.

There are many indicators of the currency of the curriculum, which assessors can draw on. These include departmental literature, curriculum committee reports, examination papers (do the same old questions keep cropping up?), teaching observation, and resources (are library holdings regularly updated?)

Academic staff are less responsive to recent developments in teaching and learning. In the case of former UFC institutions, this may be because teaching and learning has sometimes taken a back seat to research. Of course, quality assessment is changing this and will encourage a more professional approach to teaching and learning. This does not mean jumping on every educational bandwagon that comes past, but being sufficiently informed to know which to board and which to leave well alone. In order to criticize a new teaching method you need at least some foundation in educational principles. There are many areas in which it is essential for academic staff to take an interest in teaching and learning developments. For example, staff need to be aware of and responsive to changes in school curricula and teaching methods and the impact this may have on students' approaches to learning. The possible use of information technology in teaching and learning is another area that requires considered and educated evaluation, as is resource-based learning.

Assessors are not necessarily experts in teaching and learning, but at their training sessions or on other visits, they may have picked up on some of the latest developments. They might look for these during teaching observations, talking to students and so on. They might also expect something to be said about it in your departmental literature or your teaching, learning and assessment strategy. How do you develop your educational provision? What are your views on the latest developments in teaching and learning?

Good staff training in teaching and learning methods clearly helps here, along with sharing good practice. Keep up to date on changes in school curricula, possibly by involving local teachers in development of your provision. Encourage staff to periodically review their teaching methods. Set up a departmental library of educational books and material. Encourage staff to publish in one of the many teaching journals now catering for generic and subject-specific interests (Cox, 1994; Laurillard, 1993).

(i) Curricula informed by professional activities of staff

As well as teach, academic staff undertake research or other scholarly activity, and many undertake consultancy in commerce and industry. Assessors are interested in how such activities feed into the curricula. How, for example, do staff research interests inform the curriculum? Staff lecturing on their research specialisms are sometimes more enthusiastic and interesting (or incomprehensible!) Staff can include relevant examples and inspire students by exposure to the latest developments in the subject, providing valuable intrinsic motivation. While feeding research and consultancy into the curriculum, care is needed to avoid courses unreasonably biased towards the specialisms of staff. Students are entitled to a rounded view of the subject. Care must be taken to avoid unrealistic standards, which could result from staff lecturing on their research interests.

If relevant to your provision, maintain strong industrial links by inviting industrial staff to give lectures or contribute to the programme. Links with local industry and commerce can be strengthened in a number of ways, such as joint academic/industrial appointees who contribute to teaching programmes; student projects; student placements; industrial sponsorship and prizes; and research collaboration. Ensure that your links with industry are fully exploited in terms of advice on curricula and involvement of industrialists in course delivery, for example. A quote from the subject overview report for German and related languages may strike a chord here:

'there is little evidence of employer involvement in curriculum design, except in a small number of programmes which include consecutive and simultaneous interpreting in the final year. It is unrealistic of employers to expect all students to acquire business skills unless they are prepared to assist in the design of specific modules.' (HEFCE, 1996e)

Chapter 5

Teaching, learning and assessment

This chapter covers issues for teaching, learning and assessment (TLA).

1. Teaching, learning and assessment strategy

Subject level teaching, learning and assessment strategy:

(a) match of TLA activities to learning objectives
(b) match of TLA activities to curriculum (structure, content, level and mode)
(c) implications for student workload
(d) implications for student support and guidance
(e) implications for learning resources
(f) match of provision to student profile
(g) is the strategy documented and understood by staff and students?

2. Observation of teaching and learning activities

Assessors are asked to:

(h) describe the teaching and learning activities which have been observed in terms of:
   – representative sample (level, programme, mode, staff group)
   – range of sessions (eg lectures, seminars, practicals)
   – number of observations and percentage in each grade 1–4
   – range of materials for independent learning.

(i) report on the strengths and weaknesses as derived from observation notes in relation to:
   – clarity of session objectives
   – contribution of teaching (including impact of professional activity and research where relevant)

- student participation
- use of accommodation and resources
- appropriateness of sessions to the achievement of learning objectives.

3. Student assessment

(j) assessment methods: criteria, validity and reliability
(k) assessment methods and student learning
(l) feedback on students' work.

Introduction

Quality assessment evaluates the quality of the complete 'student learning experience', not just the teaching. The prominence and visibility of teaching observation during the visit may appear to contradict this. However, the interrelationships between the six aspects means that evidence from teaching observation feeds into the other aspects such as learning resources. Furthermore, TLA is only one aspect of provision and in terms of grading, is equally weighted with each of the other five aspects.

The issues for the TLA aspect outlined in the HEFCE assessors' *aide-mémoire* are divided into three sections:

1. strategy and methods for teaching, learning and assessment
2. observation of teaching and learning activities
3. student assessment.

While section 1 deals with the overall TLA strategy, sections 2 and 3 are based on the HEFCE proformas in the *Assessors' Handbook* for the observation of teaching and learning (Annex E) and the review of student work (Annex F) respectively. The HEFCE *aide-mémoire* also includes items relating to the student assessment strategy under section 3. We have moved this to Section 1 in keeping with the view that assessment should be an integral part of teaching and learning.

Teaching, learning and assessment strategies

In Chapter 3 we described the three main levels at which objectives may be set: subject/programme, course/module and teaching/classroom activity. TLA strategies can be defined at each level of this hierarchy, with links between the different levels. In this chapter we focus on TLA strategies at subject level and classroom level. The subject objectives outlined in the self-assessment state the objectives that your programmes are designed to achieve. The specific objectives which relate to the TLA aspect are called *learning objectives*. At the level of individual teaching and learning activities, assessors refer to *session objectives*.

Assessors are interested in the TLA strategies articulated by the subject provider and by teaching staff in their classroom delivery. It should be clear to assessors that the session objectives are making a contribution to the attainment of the learning objectives at subject level. They will look to the self-assessment for the learning objectives and to *you* for your session objectives. You have three opportunities to spell out your session objectives to assessors: in the briefing meeting before the observation; in the session itself; and in lesson plans that you can make available to assessors. This also applies to documented course or module objectives, which may be outlined in a student handbook. Assessors should be able to relate these to both the session and learning objectives.

How students learn

TLA strategies presuppose some understanding of how students learn. There are many theories of learning, most of which are directed at children (or dogs). The subject of adult learning is called 'androgogy' and as yet it is in a primitive state. Most quality assessment operates at a more common-sense pragmatic level. For example, *Making the Grade* (UCoSDA and Loughborough University, 1996), which incorporates some of the specialist assessor training material, discusses student learning at a fairly straightforward level and provides a compendium of principles for developing student learning. Essentially these include informing students of objectives; providing a structured content; using visual learning as much as possible; encouraging active participation; providing plenty of feedback and practice; treating students respectfully and having high expectations of them; setting realistic challenges; using a variety of methods and tasks; getting students to think and to work together; encouraging mutual support showing commitment and enthusiasm; and using a variety of assessment methods.

For the purposes of quality assessment these basic rules of thumb will probably be more useful to you than a detailed knowledge of one or other of the many theories of learning. Certainly if you demonstrate all these qualities most assessors will be perfectly satisfied. However, if you want to give more serious consideration to learning theory and want practical advice on enabling student learning, there is plenty of literature on the subject (Brown and Atkins, 1988; Cotton, 1995a, b and c; Entwistle *et al.*, 1992; Gibbs, 1992; Gow and Kember, 1993).

Teaching, learning and assessment methods

A TLA strategy should describe the teaching and learning activities used to *achieve* the learning objectives set and the assessment methods designed to *measure* them. There is a wide range of TLA methods and bearing in mind the emphasis that assessors place on variety, the following list may be of interest (Cotton, 1995a; UCoSDA and Loughborough University, 1996; Open University, 1990):

Teaching and learning

Formal lecture	A one-to-many oral presentation
Active lecture	Short sessions of student activity within a lecture
Tutorial	Small group often based on previous class, essay or problem
Exercise class	Students work through set problems with tutor assistance
Seminar	Group discussion of a paper presented by student
Role play	A portrayal or acting out of a situation
Laboratory class	Practical sessions in experimental subjects or languages
Demonstration	Practical activity to prove, illustrate or explain
Case study	Presentation of a case and working on a solution
Project	Student research with tutor providing supervision
Discussion	Groupwork sharing knowledge, ideas and opinions
Simulation	Emulation of a real-life situation
Field study	Research in the field, eg geology or biology field trip
Personal tutoring	One-to-one discussion of student's work with a tutor
Peer tutoring	Students learn from each other, within a structured format provided by a tutor
Resource-based learning	Specially prepared courseware to support student learning
Independent learning	Students work on their own, eg reading, gathering information, working through problems
Computer-aided learning	Use of computers to support learning
Distance learning	Students learn at a distance from the 'teacher'

Student assessment

Written assessment	A number of formats, eg essay, structured questions
Course work	Assignments set with opportunities for feedback
'Open book' exams	Books used in the exam to test understanding not memory

Projects	Individual or group tasks
Dissertations	Test deep understanding
Practical	A test of practical skills, eg laboratory, studio
Multiple-choice questions	Students select answer from a number of options
Single essay exams	Three-hour exam on a prepared topic
'Methods and results' exams	Writing conclusions and discussing results
Seminar presentations	Student presents work to a group
Oral exams	Interview to test oral understanding
Portfolio	Samples of student work, eg presentation and exhibition
Peer assessment	Students assess their peers against agreed criteria
Self assessment	Students assess themselves against agreed criteria
Plans and drafts	Discussion of essay plans and drafts with tutor and students
Profiles/records of achievement	Student progress log, including a range of assessment methods

What the assessors say about the TLA aspect

Assessors have commented favourably on the following (HEFCE, 1995e, 1997b; Quality Support Centre, 1996).

- The wide range of teaching, learning and assessment methods suitable for the aims and objectives and within a coherent strategy.
- The clear commitment to good teaching, including staff development.
- A willingness and enthusiasm to innovate and develop new styles of teaching and learning.
- Teaching underpinned by professional practice, scholarship and research where relevant.
- Effective links with industry, commerce and the professional and subject bodies contributing to curriculum development, good teaching practice and the development of transferable as well as subject skills.
- Effective and timely feedback to students.

On the other hand, assessors have highlighted the need to introduce effective TLA strategies, monitor assessment loads, make assessment criteria more explicit, expand the range of assessment methods used, improve feedback to students and improve the use of IT in teaching and learning.

Sources of evidence for the TLA aspect

The evidence for this aspect is largely based on the observation of teaching and learning activities and the scrutiny of student work. The details of observation are discussed later (pages 81–7), here we focus on student work. The sample of work you provide should include a range of marks, levels, specialist topics and assessment types such as coursework, examination scripts, dissertations and laboratory reports. The team will review the work in much the same way as an external examiner, looking in particular at assessment criteria, marking schemes and the quality of feedback. Are the criteria suitable and applied consistently? Have assignments been set at the right level and does the sample of student work demonstrate the achievement of learning outcomes?

Judgements made on students' work will be cross-referenced with other sources of documentary evidence, such as external examiners' reports and internal programme review documents. Assessors will talk to students about the quality of teaching and the range of TLA methods they have experienced. Note that students are *not* asked about the quality of individual classes; assessors only seek feedback on teaching in general. Agenda items for student meetings also include awareness of assessment criteria and the quality of feedback on students' work.

1. Teaching, learning and assessment strategy

What is a TLA strategy?

For HEFCE purposes, a TLA strategy should outline how the teaching, learning and assessment methods employed match intended learning outcomes, taking account of learning resources, student support issues and the student profile. It is essentially the plan for the delivery of the curriculum. The strategy might reflect the institutional mission, possibly in a code of practice. For example, an open access policy at institutional level would demand a TLA strategy that is built upon the needs of a diverse student profile.

Some providers base their strategy on key principles, such as student-centred learning or on vocational competencies. Such themes would underpin or influence the strategy; for example, in order to develop independent learning, students would require good resource-based materials, training in study and self-assessment skills, and contact time would have to be carefully targetted. Another common principle is the influence of research on teaching. Research may inform the curricula, integrate theory and practice, increase the variety of subject options and promote student enthusiasm.

Example of a TLA strategy

Your subject TLA strategy will be based on a set of objectives, which include knowledge, the application of learning, subject-specific skills and transferable skills. For the purpose of illustration we consider a selection of objectives taken from a chemical engineering programme:

- application of physical and chemical principles to the solution of practical engineering problems
- ability to conduct experiments with pilot plants
- ability to present written and oral reports of findings.

The objectives are best fulfilled by a combination of teaching and learning activities; for example, a series of lectures and small group tutorials to provide a good grounding in theory, along with laboratory classes to apply the theory and develop the required practical skills. Pilot plant workshops would serve to develop experimental skills and provide practice in report writing. Certain students, perhaps with little or no science background, might require additional tutorial support and others might require guidance on report writing and oral presentations. A range of assessment methods could be used to measure the achievement of these objectives, for example written examinations, laboratory and project reports. The pilot plant work might be assessed partly by peer assessment. Resource implications include dedicated laboratories with specialist equipment along with technical back-up and possibly postgraduate demonstrators.

This may seem like common sense, yet developing a TLA strategy can be a significant undertaking. It is not sufficient to provide a list of methods without structural relation to the objectives, and assessors have criticized this approach. The strategy might be established at institutional level; for example, a code of practice on the quality of teaching, involving a grass roots revision of curriculum planning where new and redesigned courses have to be considered in the context of the TLA strategy. The strategy also needs inbuilt QAE mechanisms, evaluating its effectiveness at subject, course and session level. Such mechanisms could include internal programme review procedures, a faculty teaching and learning committee, peer observation, student feedback and appraisal. Your strategy will evolve, so don't worry if it isn't spot on the first time around. At the very least assessors should be impressed by your efforts to formalize procedures, establish theoretical understanding and move towards a more professional approach.

Having set the scene in terms of TLA methods and strategy, we consider next the features under section 1 of the key issues for the TLA aspect. The issues (a)–(g) look at the various factors that influence the development of a TLA strategy. In each case much good practice can be found in the quality assessment reports for the subjects assessed to date.

(a) Match of TLA activities to learning objectives

In matching TLA activities to learning objectives, we first need to identify the activities that are suitable, and there could be a number of possibilities. Then we choose from these in order to construct a varied and coherent learning experience for students. The choices made at subject level will cascade down through course level and to the level of individual teaching sessions.

Learning objectives at the subject level are quite coarse and may be achieved by a wide range of activities. For example, a subject objective to develop practical skills in chemistry suggests laboratory work, the content and nature of which would be further determined by the specific practical courses included in the programme. This would have further implications at the laboratory level, where the precise experiment would be determined by the session objectives.

Strategies at all levels should be explicit and the interrelationships clear to assessors. For example, assessors of French noted that while some changes had been made in teaching and learning approaches to accommodate reduced resources and changes in degree structure, the implications for delivery by individual teachers needed more thought. In particular, many language classes are now longer than the traditional one hour, but the approach of teachers isn't always adjusted to use the additional time effectively.

An example of the hierarchy of objectives and TLA activities illustrates the above points.

> *Subject objective* – development of transferable skills, for example, time management.

At subject level, transferable skills may be developed in a number of ways, such as seminars, tutorials and fieldwork. Time management in particular may be included in a study skills course provided by the library or may be encouraged through continuous assessment and group planning exercises assessed by peer review.

> *Course objective* – ability to plan, manage, produce and present a design project within a two-term period.

The specific course objective suggests a learning activity in which time management is an integral skill. The project could be group or individual and be supplemented by tutorials and supervision. Assessment of the course objective could be via a joint project report, with peer assessment of individuals' contributions, specifically their ability to meet deadlines.

> *Session objective* – provide an outline plan of the design project including a schedule with milestones.

Constructing the plan and scheduling activities would be a session activity requiring time management skills, which might be assessed by coursework or an oral presentation.

You could adopt a systematic approach to matching learning objectives against the different types of TLA activities by constructing a grid of objectives against activities. Each objective can be considered in turn, identifying the appropriate activities to fulfil the objective, from which a suitable selection can be made. A grid might show that one of your assessment methods, such as project work, could actually measure the achievement of more objectives than at present. Having selected a number of activities you can focus on ensuring that they are properly designed and implemented to achieve or measure the objective. This approach is useful, for example, when you are planning and developing a new course.

Quality assessment reports provide plenty of examples of TLA activities that develop particular abilities or skills. For example, fieldwork provides opportunities for students to gain practical experience and to work in teams, develops a range of generic and subject-specific skills and fosters excellent staff–student relations. Effective small-group teaching provides opportunities to promote confidence, share ideas, debate issues and for students to learn how to work to a shared schedule. A range of techniques, such as team exercises and individual projects, have been recognized for developing transferable as well as subject skills. In languages, oral work, essays and report writing encourage students to master the target language, explore complex ideas and develop intellectual and presentation skills.

There are other factors to consider in selecting TLA activities, such as the many characteristics of students. For example, what previous experience do they have and what do they respond to? You may have a clear idea of the likes and dislikes of your students and this may influence your choice. Why change methods with a proven track record? The size of the group can have a big influence on the method you choose, for example the group might become too large to engage in meaningful discussion. You will also be influenced by your own preferences and skills. If you aren't sufficiently skilled in the method, do you have time to develop the required skills? Finally, there will be practical considerations such as the availability of appropriate accommodation and materials (Open University, 1990).

The literature is oddly sparse when it comes to TLA strategies in higher education, possibly because the range of teaching methods used in higher education has been somewhat limited traditionally – lectures, tutorials and laboratory classes in the main. Now the learning environment has become much richer and we have a greater range of methods available to us, including computer-aided learning, video-conferencing, computer-mediated communication, the Internet and so on. We have more students with varying backgrounds, experience and expectations. Delivery is no longer just a matter of transmitting information from lecturer to student. There is greater attention paid to independent and resource-based learning, along with much talk about student-centred and lifelong learning.

Two authors, who have done a lot of work in the design of TLA strategies, incorporating the full range of media now available to us, are Romiszowski (1988) and Laurillard (1993). Romiszowski adopts a systematic approach to instructional design whereby the selection of teaching methods and media (print, video, audio, etc) is based on the learning objectives. It takes account of other factors influencing selection such as subject matter, type of learning task and target audience.

Theories of instructional design suggest a link between what we know about student learning and what it means for teaching. Laurillard is not convinced that this link is as logical as such theories suggest. The guidance she provides on generating a teaching strategy is actually based on an analysis of what we know about how students learn, but she offers an alternative view of the learning process, ie one that considers learning as a 'conversation' between tutor and student, rather than as the transmission of knowledge from tutor to student.

Laurillard's model of the learning process is defined in terms of a dialogue between teacher and student, ie a 'conversational framework', identifying the necessary activities which make up the learning process. Essentially, interactions between teacher and student occur at the level of discussion and action, and both are able to reflect and adapt accordingly. For example, in the best scenario for learning – a one-to-one – the student can define his or her understanding of a concept, to which the teacher can respond, both can provide feedback, and the teacher can adapt his or her actions accordingly in order to achieve the desired objective.

The TLA strategy is constructed by identifying the media that can deliver the various components of this conversational framework and making an appropriate selection. The strategy must also take account of the subject and how students understand it (including their misconceptions), and address students' own beliefs about how they learn.

(b) Match of activities to curriculum

Curriculum structure and content

The TLA activities used by staff should suit what is taught and the organization of the curriculum. You would not be surprised to find a lot of individual and small-group tuition in music or fieldwork in geology. Similarly, a period abroad is a distinctive feature of language provision.

The activities should complement the way course topics have been organized. Assessors note the key role of design work in chemical engineering, promoting the integration of the different strands of the subject, as well as the development of transferable skills. Effective learning is most likely to occur when the structure and range of learning tasks build on earlier learning. For example, you might have to allow more time and provide additional tutorial support for tougher topics, or deal with underlying principles in a series of lectures before application of the theory through laboratory or design work. Highly serial subjects with many prerequisites may require regular testing of understanding, perhaps through multiple-choice tests or student presentations.

Individual TLA activities should complement each other and be integrated into the curriculum. For example, a sandwich placement or year abroad should be set in context within the programme, rather than being a discrete activity. Individual and group performance tuition for music, for example, was found to be generally very successful, but assessors did raise concerns about the relationship with the rest of the curriculum and the methods of assessment used.

Level of study

Assessors will want to know whether students can cope with the activities they are set, and if they are being appropriately challenged. For example, assessors have commented on programmes offering a number of options to students where the subject matter in years two and three isn't always substantially different in level.

If the underlying principle of a TLA strategy is student-centred learning, it might be realized by a steady progression from a high contact tutor-centred approach in the first year with lectures, tutor-led tutorials and timetabled personal tutorials to an increased level of student independence in the third year with more self and peer assessment, group work and student-led seminars. Students are likely to need training and support in the delivery of seminar presentations, or assessment of themselves and peers. These methods can be introduced gradually to build student competence and confidence.

Mode of study

It is not difficult for many pre-UFC funded universities to match TLA activities to the mode of study as the majority only have full-time mode, possibly with sandwich placement or a period abroad. However, with moves in higher education to cater for lifelong learning, different study modes will proliferate, for example, part-time and distance learning. The prime example here is the Open University, where distance learners have specially designed courseware with much self-assessment activity and targeted tutorial work.

Assessors draw particular attention to the need for better mechanisms for assessing students on work experience, placement and a year abroad. In such cases outline the specific criteria and methods for assessing their progress. Do students prepare a portfolio or a project report? Are transferable skills of students on placement assessed and recorded? What provision do you have for students returning from industrial placement or a year abroad? In particular, how do you build on their experience? For example, in French, assessment of students returning from a year abroad confirmed an increased linguistic competence, confidence and maturity, yet the skills and experiences were not always built on in a systematic way.

(c) Implications for student workload

A TLA strategy should include a planned distribution of student workload and a means of monitoring it. Is there a measure of student learning time, particularly on a modularized programme? A heavy workload and high class contact time are likely to encourage surface learning (Gibbs, 1992). Teaching staff will be aware of the workload set by their courses but are they aware of the overall workload for the programme? Is the demand steady throughout the year or clustered at the end of term or end of year? Overload of staff and students is a common weaknesses of assessment systems – students have insufficient time to complete assignments and staff to mark them. Assessment demands of different modules/courses can vary widely and sometimes there are too many assignments with the same deadline (UCoSDA and Loughborough University, 1996). This is a matter of overall programme coordination and liaison and is often a weak point in providers' TLA strategies.

(d) Implications for student support and guidance

The issue of student support and guidance is covered more fully in Chapter 7, here we make a few points about how the issues relate to the TLA strategy. Such a strategy should describe how students are supported or advised in undertaking the various learning activities. This is particularly important in the case of such methods as computer-aided learning, peer tutoring and independent learning. An area where students may require specific support is in making effective use of their private study. In French good practice in providing study skills includes a scheme for mentoring through support groups led by trained students. 'Rescue' classes are also included as part of the provision to support students experiencing difficulty with language work.

(c) Implications for learning resources

Your TLA strategy should take account of resource implications. Assessors of German found in approximately 20 per cent of cases that learning resources do not reflect the changes in teaching and learning policies, particularly the greater emphasis on independent learning. Nor have they kept pace with increasing student numbers. Similarly, many French providers aim to provide appropriate learning contexts for students to develop transferable skills and take responsibility for their own learning. However, there were only a few examples of strategies articulating how this would be achieved in terms of the necessary resources such as library, information services, specialist language equipment and courseware. There are also examples of good resources such as language laboratories and satellite television facilities being under-utilized. Do you have any measure of student usage and do you set assessment activities which necessitate the use of such facilities?

The TLA strategy should outline the resource implications for academic and support staff. Is there sufficient expertise to support the programme academically and technically, and are there effective staff development programmes in place? Assessors also comment on staff issues under the CDCO or LR aspect and staff development issues under the QAE aspect.

(f) Match provision to student profile

If your student profile is changing, assessors will be interested in the response you have made to meet the needs, particularly if it represents a wide variation in knowledge, experience and maturity. Assessors recognize that widening access can add to the difficulty of devising curricula that stretch good students while not overloading weaker ones.

Most providers of Russian and Eastern European languages and studies offer a dual entry system where the aim is to bring students new to the study, to at least A-level attainment in the first year. Then they may be taught jointly in the second year with A-level students or only brought together in the final year, after a period of study abroad. Some providers of French integrate grammar into thematic dossiers and one provider uses a grammar checklist for new entrants.

In geology assessors noted the introduction of ancillary courses in mathematics and the basic sciences in response to increased student recruitment. In a small number of cases the assessors found that weaknesses in numeracy were not fully addressed by such courses. Do you use regular diagnostic tests and feedback to ensure that students can make full use of the first year of the programme?

(g) Is the strategy documented and understood by staff and students?

Staff and students should be aware of the TLA strategy so that they understand the purpose of the various activities and tasks in which they participate. All staff involved in implementing and reviewing the strategy should have contributed to its design. If this is the case, staff are likely to be more committed to it and able to articulate the strategy to assessors.

Good learning requires high motivation and it helps if you know why you are learning something and why you are learning it in a particular way. Engineering students, for example, often complain that their mathematics is 'not relevant' because it doesn't relate to their immediate interests. It may help if they understand that they are building foundations for later on.

Students will be particularly keen to know what assessment methods you are using, when you are using them, and what they are designed to test. Make sure they understand the assessment strategy and relevant procedural details, including the units of assessment for the degree programme, the status of your course as a unit of assessment and the relationship between the units and final degree classification. Outline schedules of workload and regulations, including appeals procedures. If you have a policy on students handing in work promptly, make sure you also have one for the return of work to students. Outline procedures for internal and external moderation and mechanisms for monitoring, recording and reporting on student progress.

2. Observation of teaching and learning activities

In Chapter 2 we suggested setting up a peer review scheme for developmental purposes – observation by assessors' was not far from our minds in doing so. Peer observation for the purpose of quality assessment is a different matter and it can be a source of concern for teaching staff who are observed. The best response to is to learn as much about it as possible beforehand and to be prepared.

In fact, the HEFCE observation of teaching is quite a radical move forward in accountability in higher education provision. Despite the explicit intention of sharing good practice, there is no doubt that the judgement of teaching is being made for summative purposes. Assessors must have a notion of effective teaching in order to be able to measure it and they also expect subject providers to articulate what *they* consider to be good teaching. This doesn't mean there should be a prescription for how the curriculum is taught. Assessors will evaluate all sessions against the objectives that individual staff have set for the session, placed in the context of the subject TLA strategy.

It has been suggested that evidence gathered by assessors is not equally weighted. Teaching observation is often considered to be the most significant evidence. You can make your own mind up on this. From our experience and looking carefully at a typical visit schedule, assessors only spend about 30–40 per cent of their time during the visit engaged in observation. It appears to take up so much time because it has a direct impact on staff and is a clearly visible activity – unlike hours spent on scrutinizing documents and looking at student work.

It would appear that peer review is becoming more commonplace as a QAE mechanism. It will be interesting to see the correlation between the outcomes of this process and that from student feedback. Studies conducted in the USA provide an insight: in the evaluation of teaching, Marsh found a greater correlation between student evaluations and the self-evaluation of lecturers than there is with peer evaluation. The most significant finding is the low correlation between the judgements of different peers (Marsh, 1987). It certainly seems that the validity and reliability of judgements of individual teaching sessions cannot be taken for granted, and it is an area that needs more research.

We have to accept that the entire assessment visit is only a snapshot and the observation of individual classes equally so. However, the judgement of the quality of individual lectures is not so significant considering that the grading of the TLA aspect is based on a collective judgement of all observations, the scrutiny of students' work, feedback from students and a documented strategy on teaching learning and assessment. We look next at what you can expect from an observation in terms of the protocol that assessors must follow.

HEFCE observation protocol

Observations are predominantly undertaken by subject specialist assessors. If a reporting assessor has reason to attend a session there will be no formal observation or grade, for example, he or she might just want to get a better understanding of the particular subject context. The judgement of the quality of the session is based on the direct assessor observations. Sessions are graded on a scale of 1 to 4, with 1 the lowest and 4 the highest.

> *Grade 1.* The session fails to make an acceptable contribution to the attainment of the learning objectives set.
> *Grade 2.* The session makes an acceptable contribution to the attainment of the learning objectives, but significant improvement could be made.
> *Grade 3.* The session makes a substantial contribution to the attainment of the learning objectives, but there is scope for improvement.
> *Grade 4.* The session makes a full contribution to the attainment of the learning objectives.

Assessors *rate the session not the individual*. Individual grades are only disclosed to the lecturer being observed; they *do not* appear in the final report.

There are three stages to classroom observation by assessors:

1. briefing before the observation
2. the observation itself
3. debriefing after the observation.

Briefing before the observation

The reporting assessor supplies the local subject contact with a timetable of observations at the start of each day. If you want to know when you are going to be observed, ask! Insist on a pre-observation briefing to improve the validity and reliability of the process. It will be of mutual benefit for you to collect your assessor from the base room; this will save assessors from getting lost and it provides you with an opportunity to outline your objectives for the session. Indicate how your session fits in with what you covered last week, future sessions and how this fits in with the wider programme of study.

The observation

During the observation assessors will sit so that they can see you and the students but they should not be intrusive. They will stay for the duration of the class (unless there is a pressing reason not to) and will take notes during the observation, recording strengths and weaknesses using the observation sheet. If they can't attend the whole session or wish to talk to students in practical sessions, for example, then they should inform you. For three-hour laboratory sessions, assessors are likely to attend only a part, maybe the first and last half hour.

Assessors do not insist on seeing handouts or preparatory notes for your session, but if you want assessors to do so, make handouts available at the pre-observation briefing. Assessors do not invite student opinion on the class being observed but they do monitor student behaviour. They will notice whether students turn up on time, whether they are taking notes and listening, or whether they are switching off half-way through. Assessors have commented on students' excessive copying of notes during class time.

Feedback after the observation

After the observation the assessor must provide a brief oral feedback. If there isn't sufficient time immediately after the observation, an appointment can be made to meet your assessor later during the visit. Make sure you have this meeting; it is an opportunity for the assessor to 'offer constructive comment on the observations made rather than prescribe preferred practice' (HEFCE, 1996a).

Assessors might start by asking, 'If you did this lecture again, what would you do differently?' They provide feedback based on observations recorded using Annex E of the *Assessors' Handbook*, and give you a grade if you request it. We recommend that you ask for your grade since it may be easier in a face-to-face situation for the assessor to give you a 2 rather than a 1 or a 4 rather than a 3! The grade given has to be justified. The observation proforma is important because it constitutes part of the evidence for this aspect and may be referred to again if there are any problems or uncertainties over observation. A team decision can then be made on the basis of the evidence. Comfort might be gained from the following extract from the notes for the specialist assessor training: 'sometimes the discussion afterwards with the lecturer informs the final judgement of the class' (UCoSDA and Loughborough University, 1996).

(h) Observation of teaching and learning activities

Here assessors are asked to comment on the number and range of the sessions observed, how representative these are and the percentage in each grade 1–4. They also comment on the range of materials for independent learning if appropriate.

Observation sample

Assessors aim to see a representative sample of classes covering a variety of programmes, staff and a range of classes such as lectures, seminars, practicals and tutorials. Any teaching staff involved in provision of the subject have a good chance of being observed. This includes part-time, visiting and service lecturers as well as postgraduate teaching assistants. Don't be worried if you are observed more than once, it will be a reflection of the sampling adopted, not the grade you might be given.

Number of observations and percentages in each grade

As a rough indicator, there are likely to be at least as many observations as there are teaching staff contributing to the subject. Each activity observed is graded. Assessors calculate the percentage of each grade assigned to observations. HEFCE does not have a formula that relates the grades of classes to the overall grade for the TLA aspect.

Range of materials for independent learning

If independent learning forms a key part of the subject TLA strategy, associated learning material will provide important evidence for assessors. Make it available in the base room along with your TLA strategy. Providers of Russian and Eastern European languages and studies were commended for their imaginative use of up-to-date learning materials (some of which are produced in-house for beginners' language courses) and the highly effective use of IT and audio-visual media.

(i) Assessors report on the strengths and weaknesses observed

Annex E of the *Assessors' Handbook* invites assessors to comment on the clarity of the session objectives and the appropriateness of these to the achievement of the subject learning objectives set. Remember that assessors are building up a collective picture, each individual session does not have to relate to every learning objective. For example, an assessor may not see high levels of student participation in a particular lecture, but observations of a range of sessions could show appropriate student participation in line with the TLA strategy at subject level. Similarly, a particular activity such as a tutorial might not appear to fit in with a student-centred strategy; but there can be flexibility at the level of classroom strategies; for example, a tutorial might be tightly controlled by a tutor (almost like a mini-lecture) at one extreme, or be facilitated by a student in the absence of a tutor at the other.

Assessors also record the contribution of teaching (including the impact of professional activity and research where relevant), the extent of student participation and the use of accommodation and resources. These comments contribute to a collective judgement by the assessment team based on all observations of teaching and learning activities and they reflect the main sections of the observation form (Annex E of the *Assessors' Handbook*). They provide evidence on which to build an overall picture of the quality of teaching at subject level.

The observation sheet is used for all activities, from lecture to laboratory class. It includes the following.

- Learning objectives relevant to the teaching and learning session.
- Particular objectives planned for the session.
- Effectiveness and achievement of planned objective (planning, content, methods, pace, use of examples).
- Student participation (intention and achievement).
- Evidence of student engagement.
- Evidence that learning objectives have been achieved.
- Effectiveness of use of resources (room, specialist equipment, visual aids, IT, etc).
- Strengths and weaknesses of overall session – appropriateness of session objectives and their achievement to the overall attainment of objectives.

The above criteria are explored during assessor training since they may be interpreted in different ways by different assessors. We recommend that you try a similar exercise with your colleagues. *Making the Grade* (UCoSDA and Loughborough University, 1996) provides real examples of observed teaching sessions on video, with completed observation forms providing feedback and a grade. Group discussion of this material is guaranteed to get a debate going.

Although only one proforma is used for all types of teaching and learning activities, the assessor training material includes different criteria for different methods, for example lectures, small group teaching and laboratory sessions have the following checklists (UCoSDA and Loughborough University, 1996).

Lectures

Venue	Seating, lighting, heating, ventilation, etc?
Content	Content of lecture made clear to students?
Structure	Lecture material well organised?
Level	Could students cope with the level of material?
Clarity	Clear explanations?
Use of examples	Relevant and helpful illustrations?
Handout/materials	Appropriate use of handouts/study materials?
Audio-visual aids	Successful in supporting students' understanding?
Audibility	Could the lecturer be heard and seen by all students?
Pace and timing	Appropriately paced and to time?
Enthusiasm/interest	Student interest sustained/enhanced?
Interaction	Opportunities for questions, etc?

Small-group teaching

Skills required for small-group teaching involve preparation for both the content and the process of the session, including questioning, listening, responding, explaining and encouraging continuing interaction across the group.

Laboratory classes

Special prompts for laboratory class observation relate to organization, student involvement and the role of demonstrators.

> *Organization:* clarity of written instructions, time and equipment to complete practical work and adequacy of health and safety precautions.

Student involvement: the degree to which students are involved in their tasks and the contribution of all students to group work.

Demonstrator role: observation of students at work, assisting students, asking questions to help students' understanding, explaining procedures clearly and familiarity with the difficulties of the experiments which the students are undertaking.

What assessors have to say about observed classes

Assessors have made the following comments about the teaching they have observed based on themes emerging from subject overview reports.

- Clear aims and objectives, good planning and clear structure to the session.
- Classes characterized by enthusiastic and well-informed teaching, and consistently high quality of student contributions.
- Student contributions to discussions encouraged by tutors who provided a challenging but supportive environment.
- Much of teaching imaginative, innovative and participative and well-grounded in principles of adult learning.
- Some excellent lecturing, utilizing both 'chalk and talk' and a range of audio-visual aids.
- High levels of student interaction and participation in classes.

Conversely, some teaching was found to be repetitive, lacking inspiration and failing to challenge students. Assessors identified a need to consider more carefully the role that students play in small groups. In German, assessors identified a number of factors contributing to low student participation levels including poor preparation by students, poor pace and choice of materials, the tendency of the teacher to dominate, and failure to engage or challenge students. Similarly, for French providers, cases of 'teacher-centred' approaches were not considered to involve students or develop critical and analytical skills through independent research.

3. Student assessment

Student assessment under this aspect relates to *how* students are assessed and the role of assessment in supporting student learning, *not* the outcomes of assessment, which are covered in the SPA aspect. Other issues include consistency, fairness and feedback to students – notice there is no mention of standards. However, academic level is taken into account when assessors observe teaching and in the evaluation of student work. The QAE aspect also refers to 'comparability of qualifications', which is deemed to be assured through the external examiner system. The Welsh system refers to 'expectation of the standard of students' work' and reviewing student work constitutes a significant part of the visit. The Scottish system refers to 'standards applied in assessment schemes explicit and consistent across the curriculum'. It is clear that standards are at least an issue implicitly, even if at the moment assessors are not making any explicit references. The Joint Planning Group report (DfEE, 1996) and the Dearing Review (JPG, 1996) could change all this.

Assessors take into account many factors when judging the effectiveness of student assessment, including:

- links with the course objectives
- focus on the central aspects of what is taught and learnt
- the extent to which assessment promotes development of deep, active, reflective learning
- focus on skills and their transfer
- efficient use of assessment by lecturers
- workload for students (UCoSDA and Loughborough University, 1996).

We have already discussed the match of assessment methods to objectives, the suitability for the lecturer, the assessment of skills and the workload for staff. Here we consider the relationship of assessment and learning including the important role of feedback. First, we should remind ourselves of some key definitions in assessment.

Formative assessment is designed primarily for developmental purposes to measure student progress and provide feedback to aid learning. It does not usually contribute to students' marks or grades, allowing students to make mistakes without penalty.

Summative assessment, on the other hand, does contribute to students' marks and is designed to establish student achievement at stages throughout a programme. It represents any attempt to reach an overall description or judgement of a student to predict performance or in form selection (Cotton, 1995a; Rowntree, 1987). In practice, both forms of assessment may be used for developmental purposes.

An assessment method is *valid* if it measures what it is intended to – the aims and objectives you have set. Assessment is *reliable* if the outcome is consistent for students with the same ability, whenever the method is used, whoever is being assessed, and whoever conducts the assessment.

(j) Assessment methods: criteria, validity and reliability

Criteria

Common weaknesses of assessment systems are the undue precision and specificity of marking schemes or criteria, and students not knowing what is expected of them or what counts as a good or bad assignment (UCoSDA and Loughborough University, 1996). For every activity in which a student is engaged, assessors want to know what the intended learning outcomes are. For example, if assessors review project work, they want to know exactly what the purpose of the project is and how its achievement will be measured.

Are your assessment criteria explicit and understood by students and do they understand the rationale behind assessment weightings? For example, if a group project is marked, does this include marks for project management, an ability to work in a team and communication skills, or just the outcome of the project? Assessor training material includes examples of different approaches to the marking of group projects, which include: everyone gets the same mark; the group decides the marks for individuals at the end of the project; the group decides the criteria at the beginning and allocates marks at the end; an individual and group mark is allocated; a yellow and red card is issued – yellow for a 'malingerer' (mark reduced by 10 per cent) and a red card if there is no improvement (student gets zero). On the marking of projects assessors in chemical engineering identified inadequate differentiation of individual project marks and over-generous marking in one quarter of providers.

Are students able to distinguish between different levels of performance – do they actually know what they have to do to get a grade B for their essay? Assessors of sociology commented on the confusion caused by differing policies and practices for grading coursework.

Students can become more engaged in their learning through self-assessment. If you have a clear marking scheme and criteria, you could involve students in their own assessment as part of your formative assessment procedures. You might discuss criteria in more depth by showing students lots of examples of marked student work, such as designs or essay plans, looking at good and poorer examples and discussing the reasons for marks allocated. A small number of providers of Russian and Eastern European languages and studies have been noted for their use of self and peer assessment to help students acquire a range of transferable skills.

Validity and reliability

Student assessment should provide a valid and reliable measure of the attainment of objectives for your programmes of study. The clearer the objectives, the easier it is to ensure that assessment is valid and reliable. Again, assessment criteria that measure the learning should be clear to students so they know what is expected of them. Assessors say little about validity and reliability but do raise notions of consistency and fairness. They scrutinize students' work very carefully to determine if the work actually represents an achievement of objectives. This itself is a measure of the validity of the assessment instrument. As another measure of reliability, they consider whether the marks are appropriate and subject to moderation, internally and externally.

Wide variations in marking across and within modules/courses are considered to be common weaknesses in assessment systems (UCoSDA and Loughborough University, 1996). Reliability can be improved by peer evaluation of assessment procedures or double marking. Consider what other steps you can take to reduce subjectivity or tutor bias. For example, do you agree in advance whether criteria such as spelling and grammar should be taken into account in your marking schemes? How do you moderate oral examinations; is there a written report? Assessors of sociology comment on the reluctance of many providers to use the full range of marks, leading to the bunching of degree classifications awarded.

(k) Assessment methods and student learning

While assessors look carefully at student assessment in terms of measuring the achievement of learning outcomes, they are also interested in how you use assessment to support student learning. Is it used to provide opportunities to monitor student progress and to help students develop? Formative assessment removes the fear of failure and is an opportunity to provide timely feedback, both of which are conducive to learning. For example, a mid-term multiple-choice test can provide a quick (and coarse) measure of how students are doing, that is, if you can actually persuade students to do work that 'does not count' towards their final assessment! Assessment strongly influences both the style of learning adopted by students and motivation. For example, projects tend to promote deep understanding compared to multiple-choice questions, which tend to produce 'reproductive' styles of learning (Entwistle *et al.*, 1992; Gow and Kember, 1993).

Prompt feedback is key to formative assessment, but with time pressures, larger classes and high workload this is not always possible. You could try providing opportunities for students to assess their own work and that of their peers. Giving students some responsibility for assessment is a good way of enhancing learning, particularly since self and peer assessment are useful skills in themselves.

(l) Feedback on students' work

Assessors scrutinize carefully your feedback on student work. Would your students (or assessors) understand why the mark achieved has been allocated or how a better one could have been achieved, and is your feedback likely to encourage the students to perform well again? Do you monitor whether students respond to your feedback and are they actually learning from it? A numerical grade or a bland comment on a piece of student work is unlikely to aid learning or impress assessors. Inadequate or superficial feedback to students is a common weakness of assessment systems (UCoSDA and Loughborough University, 1996).

Are there institutional or departmental guidelines on giving feedback to students? For example, do you have an agreed timescale for students to hand in work and for staff to return marked work? If so, is it implemented consistently? Students need time to consider and respond to your feedback, so make sure it is timely; this is particularly true for modular provision. Remember, the quicker the feedback, the greater the chance that the students haven't forgotten about it!

Document as much of the feedback as you can – not just to satisfy assessors but also to benefit the students. Where you give a lot of oral feedback you may consider keeping a written record. Refer to it in the self-assessment document – the assessors will follow this up by asking students. Many providers have introduced standard proformas to encourage a consistent level of feedback. Feedback should also be sensitive. Increase student self-esteem and reduce anxiety by giving positive feedback first (Falchikov, 1995), just like feedback given by the reporting assessor.

For each student you may keep a record of achievement that documents student progression throughout the programme. This would be an invaluable record of student progression (SPA aspect). Students could be responsible for ensuring that their own records are kept up to date. It might be an idea to keep samples of student work to review your own practice, and invite a colleague to comment on your assessment of student work, as part of a peer review process.

Chapter 6

Student progression and achievement

This chapter discusses issues for student progression and achievement (SPA).

1. Student profile

(a) describe the student profile, eg typical entry qualifications
(b) match of the student profile to the aims of your subject
(c) policy and criteria for student access.

2. Progression and completion rates

(d) annual progression rates as indicators of achievement of objectives; trends in progression and completion rates
(e) procedures in place for addressing poor or non-progression
(f) transfer rates in and out of the subject
(g) qualifications awarded, eg certificate, diploma and degree results.

3. Student achievement

(h) evidence of students attaining the set objectives from their work and progression to employment or further study
(i) evidence of student achievement from external sources.

Introduction

Providers don't seem to have too much trouble with the student progression and achievement (SPA) aspect since most have long-established administrative and organizational systems in place to gather and record the sort of data required. The Quality Support Centre report (QSC, 1996) shows one of the lowest percentages of assessors' recommendations in this aspect over most subjects. However, both HEQC audit and HEFCE quality assessment have exposed a number of weaknesses arising from the impact of modularization, widening access and changing patterns of demand. Providers' record keeping and cohort analysis have not always kept pace with these developments. For example, monitoring of progression for combined and joint programmes is an area that assessors often find poor.

This aspect may become more important as changes in teaching and learning methods evolve. For example, for assessment by a developmental portfolio the monitoring and recording of students' progress and achievement would be more difficult than for an end-of-session one-off examination. An issue that might assume increasing significance under this aspect is that of *added value*. This is likely with the greater emphasis placed on the relationship between students' achievements and the initial entry status because of flexible access policies and variations in aims, objectives and entry requirements.

A particularly irksome feature of this aspect is the institutional terminology used, which could be unfamiliar to some assessors. Terms such as 'attrition' and 'retention' are not always clear from one department to another, and should probably be avoided altogether unless the institution takes a strong central line with uniform, well-defined and understood terms adopted across the institution. Otherwise, it is best to keep things as simple as possible.

Essentially, for a given programme you need a precise unambiguous definition of a cohort, ie the set of students enrolled on the programme. You then need to specify every means by which a student may enter the cohort: direct entry into first or subsequent programme years, re-entry after a break, a transfer in from another programme, either repeating a programme year or continuing normal programme year progression. Similarly, you need to specify every means by which a student can leave a cohort: successful completion, transfer out, leave of absence, repeat year, failure to re-enrol. For students who fail to complete a programme in good standing you also need the reason for this, with some agreed categorization such as required by academic failure, voluntary, for family, financial, health, work or other reasons.

There are many ways of presenting progression and achievement data, of varying degrees of transparency. The important thing is to present the data as clearly, comprehensively and accessibly as possible. As we stress throughout this chapter, particular care is needed in the case of modular and multidisciplinary provision.

What assessors say about the SPA aspect

As noted in the introduction, there is a good measure of satisfaction with this aspect. Of 272 HEFCE providers assessed in the 1995–96 round, nearly half achieved a grade 3, the other half a grade 4, and only 5 per cent were awarded a grade 2. After the SSG aspect this is the highest percentage of grade 4s. Clearly, the bulk of institutions were judged to have very good to excellent provision in this aspect. Specific items assessors identify as praiseworthy include:

- high levels of student achievement;
- high completion rates;
- progression of students to employment or further study;
- high levels of stakeholder satisfaction;
- evidence of added value;
- clear qualitative and quantitative data on applications, enrolments, completion rates and student destinations;
- monitoring trends of different types of student where relevant to the aims and objectives, for example male/female, mature, non-traditional, national and international;
- experience abroad and work experience, with appropriate preparation and learning objectives and monitoring by staff.

On the other hand, assessors have identified the need for better monitoring of student progression particularly within some modular provision (HEFCE, 1997b). They have also commented adversely on poor progression between different academic levels; unacceptably high non-completion rates (particularly in the first year of some degree courses); poorly designed access and foundation courses; difficulties in obtaining relevant employment at an appropriate level; the mismatch between the institutional mission on student access and the profile actually recruited.

Sources of evidence for the SPA aspect

Much of the evidence for this aspect is of a statistical or quantitative nature; for example, examination results, progression statistics, destination data, measures of added value and entry qualifications. It is essential that these data are presented clearly and are comprehensive enough to answer all the questions that are likely to arise. Assessors have repeatedly drawn attention to the wide variability in the nature and quality of the data that they receive. It is important to ensure that information on the progress of every student entering a given programme is complete and available. If a student does not complete a programme, or takes longer than normal over it, you should be able to explain why.

Assessors might talk to staff (particularly admissions tutors), external examiners, professional accrediting bodies, employers, and the Careers Service to gather further data. Much of the data required will be available in central administrative departments. Make sure that they match up with your departmental records.

1. Student profile

(a) Describe the student profile

There is a wide variation in the entry qualifications of students, even within a single subject. Some institutions recruit primarily from high grade A-level students, others from a broader range of 'non-standard' entry qualifications (not easily defined with the expanded university sector, but usually meaning not A-level or not direct from school), such as BTEC National Certificate, Diploma or access courses. Many institutions aim to broaden access by increasing the number of such non-standard entrants. Not all are successful: the bulk of the former UFC-funded institutions are still recruiting predominantly from A-level. In some cases foundation courses are provided for students who do not have the 'standard' entry requirements. Some HEIs now have franchise arrangements with further education colleges, or other forms of feeder courses that bring a wide range of student entry.

Ensure that the information you provide on entry qualifications is both comprehensive and easy to interpret. Use a number of statistical indicators, such as the range of entry grades and average grades. Assessors have noted that providers tend to do this meticulously for A-level entry but are less forthcoming on other qualifications, making it difficult to identify trends in non-standard entry.

Some institutions will waive high entry grades for enthusiasm and motivation, accepting students with lower grades but obvious commitment. There is also a growing trend (particularly in modern languages) to take *ab initio* students with little or no previous experience of the subject. Providers differ in how they treat such students. Some teach them separately in the first year, and phase them into the main programme in the second year. In others they may only come together in the final year. However, in many cases the successful outcome is that there is little to distinguish these students in their final degree classifications. If your student profile has such a varied entry, be sure to indicate how you accommodate the variety, and include the implications for other aspects.

An important point about entry qualifications is that they are now an unreliable indicator of the real abilities and skills profile of entrants. This is apparent in many of the languages assessed in the 1995–96 round, in which even good A-level students have a poor grasp of grammar. Similarly, even good A-level grades in mathematics are virtually meaningless as an indicator of mathematical skills. These matters are touched on elsewhere, because they have implications for other aspects. If this problem is relevant to you, indicate that you are aware of it and state what you are doing about it, for example, in terms of initial assessment and extra support.

For postgraduate programmes, entry is usually via an upper-second or first-class degree. However, particularly in the case of conversion courses, this may be in a range of different subjects, so that the profile of each student could be quite varied. Some institutions accept lower qualifications in some subjects if the student has appropriate professional experience, or alternative qualifications indicating competence to undertake the chosen programme.

Make sure that the data you provide to assessors are broken down sufficiently for them to verify statements made about your student profile. For example, if you claim to encourage access to higher education, ensure that your statistics illustrate the breakdown of entry qualifications reflecting this. Are there any measures of added value, by which outcomes from a wide variation in intake can be justified? Compare degree outcomes for non-standard entry, for example. If you have specific feeder courses, or franchise arrangements with further education institutions, how is the transition from further education to higher education handled? If there are trends in intake such as rising quality of applicants, are these understood and do you capitalize on them?

Low entry requirements will not in themselves adversely affect grading under the SPA aspect. If you have a low calibre intake, but a high quality output, this will be commended in terms of a high added value. Conversely, if Oxbridge fail a high proportion of students, despite having the highest intake standards, this must reflect poorly on the provision.

(b) Match of the student profile to the aims of your subject

Assessors are interested in how well the student profile reflects your subject aims in terms of the ratio of applications to places, entry qualifications, and the range of students. Your aims will imply something about the student profile you seek to attract. For example, you may have a policy of increasing the recruitment of female students to engineering. Does your student profile reflect this? One chemistry provider was criticized because they recruited almost exclusively from A-level candidates despite an institutional mission that emphasized widening access. In one institution a professional development scheme has been developed in conjunction with the British Computer Society, industry and the Careers Service using Enterprise in Higher Education funding. The scheme is concerned with personal, professional and career development. One would clearly expect a wide range of students for such a scheme, with a broad spectrum of background and interests.

The ratio of applications to places will give some indication of the popularity of your programme and the health of your recruitment. Assessors have often found that this statistic is not always available. Highlight any trends you are aware of and describe your response to them. Evidence from the 1995–96 round of assessments suggests that there is a growing trend in demand away from single-subject degree programmes to combined or joint honours, or institution-wide modular programmes. Also, on average, the entrants to the mixed programmes have higher entry qualifications.

Assessors consider trends in recruitment levels. Where recruitment has fallen, what has been done about it? Some providers respond by lowering entry standards or increasing the range of courses and options. Sometimes it works the other way with sudden unexplained increases in demand. Applications to chemical engineering have increased considerably in recent years, which may be related to the relative success in recruiting female students (HEFCE, 1996f). Applications to postgraduate programmes are low in some subjects, with vocationally oriented programmes faring best.

Sometimes, when a subject is not commonly taught at schools, such as Italian, qualifications in related subjects must be accepted and the main subject taught *ab initio*. In this case the link between aims and entry qualifications needs careful explanation: essentially all of the entrants are 'non-standard'. Former PCFC-funded institutions tend to have the most diverse entry qualifications.

Assessors will require clear statistics on the range of students recruited, in terms of age, gender, ethnicity, disability and so on. Many subjects plan to increase recruitment of mature students, a trend that is almost certain to continue with the move towards the need for lifelong learning. Sociology providers are keen to recruit mature students because they often have useful experience that can benefit the other students. The proportion of mature students in this case varies between 10 per cent and 50 per cent of the intake. Assessors have noted that very little information is forthcoming on ethnic minorities in the statistics they receive on student profiles. The key point is that you are aware of the student mix, have good, accessible data on it, and are both accommodating to it in your provision and take advantage of any benefits it brings.

(c) Policy and criteria for student access

You might have strict entry requirements – three As at A-level for example – in which case your policy on access is simple. However, many institutions, driven by the need to increase student numbers or by the general move to widen access, might have more liberal arrangements. Increasing access implies the need for more proactive measures to encourage students to take up offers, for example *ab initio* facilities, individual interviews and increased flexibility in course choice. Some departments have links and franchise agreements with local colleges as a means of increasing access. Staff should be clear on policy and prospective students on entry requirements, preferably through a documented policy for admissions tutors and students. The access arrangements should be clear and public.

It is particularly important to match up your access criteria with appropriate provision. If student access is broadened, there must be measures in place to ensure a good success rate for the atypical student entry. Some sort of initial assessment might be necessary to determine the usual 'starting point' for a wide range of student abilities. In sociology, for example, the high recruitment of mature students is often matched by appropriate support in terms of study-skills development, crèche facilities and timetables to suit family commitments.

2. Progression and completion rates

(d) Annual progression rates as indicators of achievement of objectives; trends in progression and completion rates

The main point is whether your annual progression rates are recorded in a sufficiently transparent way. Assessors have found this to be a weak area in some institutions. Even if they are recorded properly and are clear to understand, if failure rates are high, assessors will want to know why. Assessors have found that while statistics provided for single-subject provision are often clear, this is much less so for combined, joint and modular provision, where the responsibility for monitoring progression is not always clearly identified. This is a common problem and one that you would be well-advised to address. Poor data on progression are also highlighted as a particular weakness of some self-assessments under the QAE aspect.

To investigate whether progression rates indicate achievement of objectives, assessors first have to be satisfied that the methods of assessment are valid and reliable measures of attainment of the objectives. Clearly, the progression rates might look fine, but if the assessment procedures themselves are flawed, there can be no certainty that the objectives have been achieved.

This problem is evident in some of the subject overview reports for the 1995–96 round. Assessors in Italian claim that the attainment of intended outcomes is indicated in the level of final degree performance. However, at the same time for more able students they question the level of challenge that these results reflect, ie a low number of first-class degrees despite high intake quality. The point is that the degree classifications awarded must be compared with the student work scrutinized. The French subject overview report contains some good practice in this respect, while in German it was noted that scrutiny of students' work indicates that achievement by students is 'more variable than the... degree results profile would tend to indicate'.

Assessors commend high levels of student achievement in terms of completion rates and qualifications. They are impressed by good completion rates against a background of recruitment of a high proportion of non-standard entrants (good added value). However, concern has been expressed about the lack of a clear definition of the concept of added value – many claim it, but few provide supporting evidence. An instance of apparent 'subtracted value' has emerged in the 1995–96 round, in which, for example, combined honours students are sometimes attaining lower degree results despite higher entry qualifications. The reasons for this are not clear but could be related to the non-linearity of combined subjects – 'half plus half' is greater than 'one'. Some language providers claim good added value for *ab initio* and mature students, with their final degree classifications frequently indistinguishable from the achievements of other students.

High completion rates are often associated with high levels of student support. Similarly, examples of recommendations for avoiding high non-completion rates (more than 10 per cent) for first-year students include the simplification of the tutoring scheme and the provision of regular meetings. In some cases there is a need to: monitor student progression more carefully, provide students with more effective feedback on their performance, and consider means of improving progression rates. Assessors have expressed particular concern about high failure rates for progression beyond the first or second year in some engineering subjects, for example chemical engineering. This is becoming a common problem in engineering, probably because of the growing difficulties experienced at the secondary/tertiary interface. In general, assessors have particularly recommended the monitoring and improvement of progression and completion rates for weaker students on joint honours programmes, students in early stages of modular schemes, students on first-year courses, and final-year projects.

Particular attention needs to be given to statistical indicators in the case of modular programmes. Assessors should be able to determine who is in the programme, who is not and who might be taking a module on a one-off basis. Progression through and between modules, and annual progression through modular provision, also need effective monitoring. It is important to try to make sense of this for assessors. You can describe modular provision and associated monitoring mechanisms in an annex to the self-assessment.

Higher education institutions are in a privileged position: they validate, set and mark their own examinations. Progression and completion rates are largely in the hands of the subject provider, who is therefore solely responsible for trends such as grade inflation or increasing failure rates, unlike their counterparts in schools where trends might be imposed on them by changes in national examinations. Assessors will look for explanations of such trends, and will expect the provider to investigate them and take appropriate action. When the first cohort passing through GCSE arrived at universities their more varied backgrounds took some departments by surprise, leading to poor first-year results. Alert departments would have anticipated the impact that changes in the school curriculum would have, and would have been better prepared.

(e) Procedures in place for addressing poor or non-progression

Disturbingly, the 1995–96 round of assessments revealed significant numbers of providers with inadequate procedures for addressing poor progression, especially for shared and modular provision. If your progression rates are poor, it is no good blaming the students; this is solely the subject providers' responsibility. It may be that there is insufficient academic support for students, or that the workload is too high. Whatever the reason, assessors will expect you to have identified the problem and considered how best to deal with it. They will look for good record keeping that promptly identifies problem areas and students' difficulties. They will want to see mechanisms for addressing such problems with clear lines of responsibility. These should be documented in departmental literature, such as a student handbook.

Keep records for each student, giving reasons for poor progression, action taken to remedy this and so on. Ensure a quick, focused response as soon as problems are detected. Personal tutors should debrief students on their assessment results, advising them of their options. Regular coursework and feedback will help detect problems before they translate into examination failure and non-progression. The subject overview report for Iberian languages and studies records the use of 'progression committees' in monitoring progression. The value of these is reflected in excellent progression, particularly in the case of well-supported *ab initio* provision. Similarly, good record keeping on withdrawals is commended by assessors of linguistics. Some French providers are now setting minimum attendance levels for successful completion of course units and are introducing electronic monitoring of students' progress and performance.

(f) Transfer rates in and out of the subject

Yet again, assessors bemoan poor statistics and record keeping in transfer rates in combined and modular provision. Often, the presentation of cohort statistics makes it difficult to keep track of transfer rates and sometimes reasons for transfer are not identified. Assessors frequently experienced difficulty determining precisely how many students had withdrawn, transferred or failed courses. There may also be a conflict between terminology at departmental level and institutional level; for example, transfer from one department to another *within the institution*, would be regarded as attrition by the department, but not by the institution. This comes back to the central problem of making cohort statistics transparent and easy to understand.

Transfers in and out of programmes give a clear indication of students' satisfaction with the provision – they vote with their feet. Trends in this area are therefore particularly significant. In the 1995–96 round, for example, some providers in Italian were benefiting from transfers in, while some Russian providers were suffering net losses of students.

(g) Qualifications awarded, eg certificate, diploma and degree results

Assessors note that good data are usually available here, allowing them to spot recent trends and any anomalous features. What will attract assessors' attention here is if the distribution of awards looks unusual, for example a cluster of first-class degrees. Achievement will also be set in context, ie consideration given to the input (student profile) as well as the output. We have already mentioned under issue (d) (pages 98–99) that assessors are interested in evidence of added value, which may be manifested in good final results against a background of variable intake. In French, assessors found cases of graduates who entered without academic qualifications gaining honours degrees. On the other hand, they found that some of the most able students were not stretched. Both assessors and teachers felt that changes to procedures for arriving at degree classifications had reduced the proportion of first-class degrees awarded.

Of interest in regard to trends in degree awards is a report commissioned by HEQC from Professor Keith Chapman of the University of Aberdeen (HEQC, 1996c). This considers the pattern of degree awards in eight subjects (accountancy, biology, civil engineering, French, history, mathematics, physics and politics) at mainly pre-1992 universities over the period 1972–1993. Among other things it found a clear trend over time for an increasing proportion of 'good honours' degrees to be awarded. This report is clearly relevant to this particular issue.

3. Student achievement

(h) Evidence of students attaining the set objectives from their work and progression to employment or further study

Assessors will look at students' work, destination data for employment and further study, cohort statistics, examination results and coursework, staff and student meetings, external examiners' reports, and teaching observation.

Assessors' comments on student work will relate to the whole range of activities, including written, oral, laboratory, industrial placement, period abroad, personal development and transferable skills – ie anything that forms part of the educational experience. Student work should give an idea of the extent to which the subject objectives are met, provided that student assessment is valid and reliable and that there is a relationship between objectives from course to subject level. For example, if one objective is the development of good IT skills, then there should be evidence of this in student work, such as coursework or projects. A specific proforma is used to evaluate student work (Annex F, HEFCE, 1996a), including suitability to the objectives and to curricula. As always the development of transferable skills comes in for particular attention in most subjects. Scrutiny of student work often leaves assessors impressed in many aspects of transferable skills, but one which does seem to give particular cause for concern is IT (see Chapter 4).

If your objectives declare intentions to prepare students for particular types of employment, to fulfil a national need in some area or to go on to further study, assessors would expect this to be reflected in your destination data. For example, if you have a programme in ophthalmology it would be odd if all your students went into accountancy. Destination data are often poor, with inadequate monitoring of careers and employment, especially for postgraduate programmes. Assessors have noted a need to gather data over a longer period of time, particularly for humanities and arts programmes, as first destinations might not be a true reflection of employment (the first job might be a summer job). Keep in touch with your graduates, and keep track of what they are doing. One institution was commended for receiving feedback from past students five years after graduation.

The employment record for full-time students of business and management (assessed in the 1993–95 round) was considered to be very good, given the economic climate. For such providers more than 50 per cent of students find jobs or postgraduate places, although in most it is nearer 75 per cent and in some as high as 90 per cent. Similarly, most subjects assessed in the 1995–96 round have good employment records, in a diverse range of careers. Some subjects have well-established vocational routes, such as the teaching profession. The job prospects of students are significantly enhanced in institutions with good links with industry, for example in chemical engineering.

(i) Evidence of student achievement from external sources

Evidence can come from external examiners' reports, professional/validating bodies, employers/professional practitioners and graduates; all of these sources provide valuable feedback on student achievement. This is the sort of material that might be referred to in the self-assessment, but with further information provided during the visit. It is simply a matter of keeping good records and being proactive about getting the information. Placement reports from employers are a useful source of information on sandwich students. Assessors are likely to meet with a selection of employers, and might actually visit industrial placements if it is a key part of your provision. Try to accommodate this, as it could provide valuable evidence.

Quality audit has identified the need for a review of the external examiner system. The important thing is to make it easy for the external examiner to provide the sort of evidence that will be useful in quality assessment, perhaps by providing a proforma related to issues of student achievement, or indeed any issue on which the examiner is qualified (and willing) to comment.

Interestingly, quality assessment reports make little reference to input by professional/validating bodies and employers/professional practitioners as evidence of student achievement. (Italian is an exception, where the employers and professional body representatives interviewed spoke highly of students.) Assessors are likely to request a meeting with a sample of past students. The Careers Service might be able to help here, or your institution might have an alumni officer. Graduates are usually supportive of their *alma mater*, often commending their programmes as providing good preparation for the world of work. Certainly, in the 1995–96 round graduates interviewed were highly complimentary about their educational experience.

Chapter 7

Student support and guidance

This chapter covers issues for student support and guidance (SSG):

(a) student support and guidance strategy
(b) documentation provided for students
(c) identifying and meeting individual student needs
(d) departmental and institutional provision
(e) staff–student relations
(f) arrangements for student admission and induction
(g) arrangements for academic guidance and tutoring
(h) arrangements for pastoral and welfare support
(i) arrangements for career guidance.

Introduction

The student support and guidance (SSG) aspect relates to both academic and pastoral matters. It includes support of students off campus in such activities as field studies, work experience and study abroad. It also includes support provided by central services such as careers, welfare groups, health and counselling.

Reductions in staff and increasing student numbers have put pressure on the personal tutoring system and staff now have less time to spend with their students. At the same time, the personal and academic pressures on students are increasing. A recent study by Evelyn Marks discloses the seriousness of support issues for students, most of which are related to study rather than cash (Marks, 1996). This might reflect the increasing numbers entering higher education, and a larger proportion who are not able to cope with the traditional expectations of university students. However, despite the pressures on the unit of resource, the outcomes of quality assessment for this aspect are impressive. Assessors of sociology commend the high level of individual support for learning through personal tutors and informal contacts, despite the increase in student numbers and smaller staff to student ratios.

What the assessors say about the SSG aspect

Quality assessment outcomes show a massive vote of confidence in the support and guidance given to students in HEIs, with 72 per cent of providers achieving a grade 4. This aspect also achieved the lowest percentage of grade 2s. Particular characteristics of high quality education in this aspect include:

- comprehensive and effective student support systems, well matched to the size and nature of its intake;
- high quality staff–student relations, which have a positive impact on student learning;
- effective links between subject and institutional central services. (HEFCE, 1997b)

The only major weakness identified by assessors relates to the support of students off-campus – on work experience, on placement or a period abroad. Can support systems be so effective against a background of severe strain on resources? It might be that staff are managing to achieve high levels of support against the odds, or perhaps peer assessors take into account the current climate in higher education and reward valiant efforts. Maybe the findings themselves do not in fact represent a valid measure of this aspect. Assessors might be able to determine whether mechanisms (such as counselling) are in place, but do they have the professional expertise to make a judgement on the effectiveness of such provision in meeting the objectives set? Certainly, in our experience meetings with central services are conducted with varying degrees of rigour. For example, some represent no more than an informal chat and others have been highly structured and required hard statistics.

One might also ask what benchmarks assessors are using to inform their judgement. They are likely to be judging against their own norms originating from their own experiences in the system (this can apply to all aspects of provision, of course).

Sources of evidence for the SSG aspect

Student support and guidance includes both departmental and institutional provision. Central services are usually visited by one or two assessors touring departments for about two to three hours in total. This is not a lot of time and it means, for example, that the Students' Guild or the Careers Service may only receive a 15-minute visit. However, it is clear that assessors aim to gain an overall impression of the quality of support services, rather than judging the quality of individual services per se.

Assessors will review departmental and institutional literature such as student handbooks and induction material, and guidance on specific activities such as project and fieldwork. Students will be invited to comment on the support and guidance they receive including: admission and induction procedures, the quality of written guidance, arrangements for academic and pastoral support, and support during study abroad and work experience.

(a) Student support and guidance strategy

The HEFCE *aide-mémoire* refers to a strategy for student support and guidance and a specific set of objectives for this aspect might be expected. However, views on this are mixed. Assessors of French note that few institutions have aims and objectives specifically referring to support and guidance, but in general such support is implicit and underpins the aims and objectives relating to progression and achievement. In contrast, we know of an assessment during which the assessors expressed surprise that high quality support was not stated as an aim of the department, considering the high-quality of provision in that area.

You could choose to integrate support and guidance issues into your TLA strategy or outline the aims for this aspect in a separate SSG strategy. However you choose to present the strategy, ensure that it outlines how the support needs of all student groups are identified and how the needs are met. You should outline the provision available, lines of responsibility, how the services are monitored and how students are informed of the services available. Describe the specific procedures for student admission and induction, pastoral and welfare support, academic and personal tutorials and careers advice. Include provision by central services such as welfare, health and counselling services. Don't forget help and guidance from secretarial and technical staff. The involvement of such staff in the support of students has been commended by assessors in the most recent HEFCE report (1997b). Outline the mechanisms available to students to provide feedback on support and guidance provision and, where available, evidence that feedback has been responded to.

The student profile may be quite diverse, for example it may include over-seas, part-time, distance learning, standard and non-standard entry, under-graduate, postgraduate and mature students. Each may have a range of needs relating to study, health, employment, financial matters and social integration. Some of the needs can be anticipated and appropriate arrange-ments planned; for example, if you have an access policy that actively recruits non-standard entrants, both the curriculum and TLA strategy can be adapted accordingly. Other needs can only be identified as the progression of students is monitored throughout the programme via personal tutorial meetings and diagnostic tests, for example.

If the institution has a policy on student support and guidance or equal opportunities, state how your departmental procedures complement these. Assessors in German noted that about one-third of providers catered well for the needs of particular student groups including part-time, non-standard entry, mature and disabled, but only one report made explicit reference to equal opportunities.

(b) Documentation provided for students

The documentation you provide for students represents a key source of evi-dence for assessors, as they can see how you describe your provision to stu-dents. It is useful to list every item of documentation that you give to students, including handbooks, guides, leaflets and one-off handouts. The student handbook is likely to be a key document scrutinized by assessors, along with codes of practice, a student charter and specific leaflets on support services. Consider other forms of communication with students, such as a notice board or electronic mail. Outline the arrangements for communicating with your students in the SSG strategy and ensure that the needs of all stu-dents are represented. In French, assessors noted that the quantity and quality of information provided for postgraduate students was inferior to that provided for undergraduates.

Assessors commended comprehensive documentation given to students at the start of a course. Examples include the aims and objectives of the course, course syllabuses and assessment, departmental expectations, deadlines for assessed work, reading lists, support systems and central services.

(c) Identifying and meeting individual student needs

The mechanisms that you use to identify and meet student needs should be included in your SSG strategy. The student profile and their associated needs may be quite diverse. It may be helpful to list the main categories of need in a grid and match them against a list of support services. As a preparatory exercise before the visit, you could invite students to complete the grid themselves to determine whether students are fully aware of the services available to them.

Ensure that your provision is able to meet students' needs. Assessors have commended a range of support mechanisms, including: child care facilities for mature students with families; study skills and 'remedial' support for non-traditional students; a special needs coordinator for students with disabilities. Good examples of 'remedial' support include diagnostic tests at an early stage in the course, a scheme for mentoring through support groups led by trained students, and 'rescue classes' where students who are encountering difficulties can negotiate the syllabus.

On the other hand, the need for extra tuition in mathematics, IT and language options was identified by assessors. Assessors commend the additional support for students with non-traditional qualifications on some applied social work courses, although provision was considered to be somewhat variable. In chemical engineering, assessors recommended that providers with increasing numbers of non-traditional students should monitor their attendance at tutorials and review student progress more regularly. Assessors have often found support for part-time students and postgraduates to be poor. For some chemical engineering providers, postgraduate students experienced more difficulty than undergraduates in gaining access to personal tutors. Assessors felt that this might reflect a misconception that postgraduates need less help.

Where you provide additional support for specific students, what evidence do you have that it is working? Do those students who would benefit most from the provision actually make use of it? Assessors found examples of weaker students failing to take advantage of 'remedial' tutorials. If you provide extra support for students, monitor the success of the provision closely, perhaps through regular personal tutorial meetings.

Assessors of Italian noted a variation in the extent to which students use central services. Do you know how well your students use such services and what they think of them? Students might have opportunities to provide feedback on the support and guidance they receive, for example, termly interviews with students or informal discussion in tutorials. If there are standard procedures for monitoring student admission procedures, open days and induction, make sure students are aware of them and, if appropriate, outline issues that have been addressed in the past.

(d) Departmental and institutional provision

Students should be aware of the support provision available both within the department and centrally. Departmental sources include academic, secretarial, administrative and technical staff, as well as other students and departmental literature. Central services include the Health Centre,

Counselling, Residences, Student Welfare, Finance, the Students' Guild, Careers and Physical Recreation. The Library and Computing Services have a supporting role but these are dealt with under the LR aspect.

Ensure that you have evidence of the link between your provision at departmental level and that provided centrally. Invariably, the central services commended by assessors have effective links with subject staff at departmental level. What liaison mechanisms do you have to ensure that student needs are identified and addressed? Do staff have official roles, or is liaison informal, relying on the goodwill and dedication of a few staff? Do students know who is responsible for what? A number of sociology providers have a one-stop support service, ie one location for all students' needs. Assessors noted that in this case the support services were well used because students found it easier to visit and discuss their problems in context. Review your current procedures for liaising with central support services and consult with them in your preparations for quality assessment. You could consider ways of formalizing the links to optimize the support available for your students. Are central support services familiar with the needs of *your* students?

Central services should be able to provide statistics on the level of student usage and indicate how students gain access to them, for example by self-referral or referral from your department. Are there specific procedures for referring students to central services? Assessors might ask for statistics on student usage of central services and consider these in the context of your student profile. One assessor in an electrical engineering department of predominantly male students asked whether the counselling service saw many female students!

(e) Staff–student relations

Assessors comment favourably on staff–student relations and refer to the 'ethos of care and support', the 'sense of academic community' and a 'shared commitment between staff and students to the study of the subject'. Good working relations between staff and students enhance the effectiveness of student support mechanisms. For example, assessors commend good staff–student relations where students feel sufficiently comfortable to approach academic staff within the department on academic matters, in addition to their personal tutor. For social policy and administration, student support was identified as a key contributory factor in promoting the quality of the student experience.

(f) Arrangements for student admission and induction

This includes information and advice to students during the application, enrolment and induction phases. Document your procedures for open days, student admission and induction at departmental level including the role of central services in these processes, for example, Schools Liaison, Registry, Careers and the Students' Guild. Linguistics assessors commended the time staff invested in interviewing all short-listed candidates. This policy is based on an interest in students' enthusiasm for the subject as well as his or her academic ability.

In outlining your procedures include the role of the admissions tutor, documentation for students, management of open days, arrangements for induction, and mechanisms for monitoring the effectiveness of the procedures, such as staff–student committees. Talk to Schools Liaison and other central services about the feedback they gather on open days and admissions procedures. If you issue information packs to prospective students, teachers and careers advisers on open days, make these available in the base room.

Lago and Shipton (1995) argue that induction and orientation into higher education is becoming more important, as the range of students becomes more diverse and higher education provision more complex with more curricular options and modes of study. Second-year students might be able to comment more effectively on enrolment and induction, indicating the relevance and suitability of the procedures. You could involve second- and third-year students in designing an induction pack – they will know what would have been useful to them when they first started. Current students are frequently involved in induction as guides and mentors. Some providers organize a separate induction for postgraduate students and targeted activities for mature students. Assessors have commended induction that is tailored to the needs of undergraduate and postgraduate students. This is also mentioned under the broad characteristics of high-quality education (HEFCE, 1997b).

Do your induction programmes cover more than an introduction to the course and the institution? What provision is there for staff–student and student–student introductions at a personal level? Lago and Shipton (1995) stress the importance of the latter to help students feel at home and reduce the feelings of social isolation. They provide a four-stage model for induction to help staff in preparation for such activities. These are pre-arrival induction (welcome letters, open days, interviews); day of arrival induction (contact with contemporaries might be useful); overall introduction to the course, facilities and staff (opportunities for formal meetings between staff and students and to explain the purpose of lectures, tutorials projects, etc); and ongoing induction in which new subjects are introduced.

Lago and Shipton also outline structured forms of 'introductions' including social and sporting events, peer support and buddy systems. For Iberian languages and studies assessors commend open days that are supplemented by a week of induction. The induction includes meetings with academic staff, the distribution of course materials and social integration.

(g) Arrangements for academic guidance and tutoring

There is an important distinction between educational tutoring and counselling (Jones *et al.*, 1997). The former is the responsibility of every lecturer but the latter might be best dealt with by the Counselling Service. Are academic staff trained in identifying student concerns that are non-academic and able to refer them to the appropriate support service?

What are the arrangements for academic tutoring in your institution and department? The purpose of academic tutorials should be clear to staff and students and preferably documented. Such provision is best outlined in the subject TLA strategy since it is key to student learning. For about one-third of chemical engineering providers, assessors recommended strengthening the commitment to formal and compulsory tutorials. In some cases it was considered that the lack of academic tutorials could contribute to high non-completion rates. A major problem with tutorials is one of attendance – what efforts do you make to ensure that students attend tutorials? Some French providers have set minimal attendance requirements.

How do your academic tutorials support student learning and enable student difficulties to be identified and addressed? Assessors will probably observe a range of academic tutorials and can judge the quality of this support for themselves. They will not be able to observe one-off 'knock on the door' consultations, but they can ask students about the availability of staff and the quality of the help they receive. Make sure you have a chance to talk to assessors about this, so that they do not get a one-sided view from students. A policy document or handout would be helpful; assessors might want to know how often tutorials are run, whether they are compulsory or optional, if students are assessed in tutorials and how the effectiveness of tutorials is monitored.

Describe the nature of academic guidance for students in the self-assessment and give examples, such as preparation for key pieces of work (eg first experiences of assignments, examinations and dissertations), and important learning activities such as industrial placement or final-year project work. Consider what other forms of guidance students are given, such as advice on curricular and vocational matters relating to decisions about options and project work, or specific support for preparing students for the next stage of study. If project work is a key activity, outline the nature of tutorial support and supervision.

Assessors might visit students on placement to determine if their support requirements are being addressed. They identified the need for better support mechanisms for students on work experience, placements and a period abroad (HEFCE, 1997b). Examples of good practice in preparing students for such activities include briefings, regular monitoring, supervision and debriefing sessions on return; comprehensive written and audio-visual supporting material; and drawing from experiences of other students. Some institutions have effective links with a network of contact people in universities, colleges and firms of the placement country. Staff keep in touch with students in a variety of ways, including visits to host institutions, letters, telephone and e-mail.

(h) Arrangements for pastoral and welfare support

Assessors review pastoral and welfare support at departmental level and that provided centrally, including health, welfare, financial advice and counselling. Does the SSG strategy provide a comprehensive description of all the provision available to students for pastoral support? How do students get to know about it? You could describe, or possibly illustrate on a flow diagram, the channels by which pastoral and welfare support are accessed, and make this available during the visit. You could also include departmental literature and leaflets produced by central support services.

Assessors will review your personal tutoring policy and its effectiveness. The personal tutoring system is often the cornerstone of the strategy for student support and guidance – providing both academic and pastoral support. Practice varies, including open-door policies, surgery hours and regular fixed appointments. If you have a personal tutoring policy, staff should be aware of it; they need to be clear about the purpose, scope and methods of the system to ensure consistency of provision. Students will be aware of whether staff vary in their practice, and it may become clear to assessors.

It is widely recognized that personal tutoring systems have come under pressure since the late 1980s with increasing student numbers (Lago and Shipton, 1995; Jones *et al.*, 1997) and assessors will be aware of this too. They will be interested to see how you are coping. There is also a recognition that the role of tutor is a complex one and that staff rarely receive training.

Is provision consistent across levels of study and, if so, do students have the same personal tutor throughout their period of study? In particular, considerable variation was found in the provision of personal tutoring for students on modular programmes. In some cases assessors have recommended personal tutoring be extended beyond the first year in order to ensure continuity for students. In others, personal tutoring systems could be more formalized and proactive. Good examples include systems supported by detailed guidelines and with good communication between staff and students, enabling prompt action to be taken when students encounter difficulties. Don't worry about 'informal' meetings with students: assessors do recognize the importance of these to supplement more formal activities. Poorer provision was generally the result of high student numbers or increased pressure on staff time, leading to an unmanageable level of demand on tutors.

Assessors are likely to check the reality of an open-door policy for themselves. Are staff in fact available on this basis and do students actually make use of it? Is the system tutor-led with regular and planned meetings or student-led with students making the first approach? Consider how you inform students of the personal tutoring system; is it outlined in the student handbook? Students need to know what to expect from the system, who to go to as a first point of contact, the frequency and nature of meetings and the mechanisms by which they can provide feedback on the provision they receive.

(i) Arrangements for career guidance

Assessors review provision from the central Careers Service and specific provision or advice provided for students at departmental level. How are students informed of such provision – is it in the Student Handbook, do the Careers Service provide relevant literature or do individual students have to find out for themselves? Assessors will consider the relevance of the careers advice to the curriculum, including any study abroad or industrial placement. Your subject aims and objectives might have implications for such provision, for example curricula with a strong European component or a highly vocational subject, such as engineering or pharmacy. Assessors of architecture identified the need to provide support for students who wish to follow less specialized careers. For sociology the quality of information about careers is considered inadequate in most cases. However, assessors do recognize that some institutions are paying attention to improving these services and to the importance of transferable skills such as numeracy, literacy and communication valued by students in their current employment.

Another area for consideration is the support and guidance in preparation for employment. To what extent are commercial and industrial contacts of staff used to help graduates find employment? Assessors have noted good practice where Careers Services are active in organization workshops on writing a CV, interview techniques and personality and aptitude tests. They may also collaborate on arrangements for the period abroad to optimize the possibility of subsequent employment. Careers literature and employer statistics will be scrutinized. You could provide feedback from students and testimonials from employers in the base room.

Assessors will talk to students, graduates and the Careers Service. Can your Careers Service provide statistics on student usage and does it seek student feedback on the service? If your institution has an alumni officer, make sure you make the most of this valuable resource. He or she could help you coordinate and gather feedback from graduates to make available to assessors and bring together a sample of students to talk to assessors on the visit.

Chapter 8

Learning resources

This chapter addresses issues for learning resources (LR).

1. Strategy

(a) learning resources strategy
(b) liaison with central services and departmental support staff.

2. Library resources

(c) availability and accessibility to all students
(d) induction and ongoing user support
(e) books, periodical stocks, learning packs and study spaces.

3. Equipment and IT

(f) availability and accessibility, including arrangements for students to work independently
(g) general and specialist equipment
(h) learning materials, for example Teaching and Learning Technology Programme (TLTP)
(i) induction and ongoing user support.

4. Teaching and social accommodation

(j) suitability of teaching, social, dining and recreational accommodation.

5. Technical and administrative support

(k) technical and administrative support for utilization of learning resources.

Introduction

Here you are asked to describe and provide evidence of how your resources are *deployed* to support learning – the factual statement of the resources is given in the framework section of the self-assessment document. HEFCE states clearly that the key to the learning resources (LR) aspect is the extent to which the appropriate resources are available and effectively used to support learning, not the resources per se. In recent years the range of resources available has resulted in a richer environment for learning; traditional resources such as library and textbooks are now supplemented with IT, audio-visual and multimedia resources. The resource environment may also include learning space, teaching and support staff, museums, galleries, and local industry (Higgins *et al.*, 1996).

Library and computing issues feature prominently under the LR aspect. A taskforce of library and computing services professionals was set up to prepare an *aide-mémoire* for quality assessors to aid evaluation of these services on the assessment visit. The taskforce included representatives of the Standing Conference of National and University Libraries (SCONUL) and the University and Colleges Information Systems Association (UCISA). The *aide-mémoire*, which has been sent to reporting assessors and has been incorporated into the specialist training of quality assessors, is reproduced in Appendix II. It provides a general checklist of issues to be explored with the library and computing services, academic staff and students.

Comments on staff issues tend to appear under three aspects:

- CDCO – matching staff expertise to the curriculum;
- SSG – good staff–student relations;
- LR – staff profile and deployment.

Staffing is an important issue. It was the key concern of assessors allocating a grade 1 under the LR aspect for two providers of modern languages including German and related languages. In fact, in a quarter of German providers (single subject) assessors judged the number of teaching staff to be insufficient and the deployment of staff to be ineffective. They also found there to be more part-time than full-time staff and undue administrative pressures on full-time staff.

The outcomes of quality assessment might be considered to undermine the view that judgement is based on the *deployment* of resources alone. For providers assessed between 1992–95 'excellent' provision is concentrated in relatively prosperous institutions (HEFCE, 1995e). For purposes of analysis HEFCE measured 'institutional prosperity' in terms of total income per student. The caveat to this is the lack of funding measures at subject level.

HEFCE also argues that institutions have many sources of income (not just from the funding council) and income says nothing of expenditure in an institution or on a subject.

Naturally, high quality accommodation, equipment and learning support facilities will have a positive impact on the student experience, but assessors have observed excellent practice in institutions with relatively poor resources. Similarly, departments may have ample resources but use them ineffectively. Remember that the aims and objectives you have outlined in the self-assessment should be set in the context of your resources. There is no point setting objectives that you cannot resource; objectives must be achievable.

What the assessors say about the LR aspect

Assessors seem fairly satisfied with this aspect. Some specific comments include the following.

- Well-resourced teaching accommodation, good IT and library provision, suitable equipment, with effective deployment of and access to resources as part of an overall teaching and learning strategy.
- Classrooms are fully equipped, spacious and flexible to accommodate a diversity of uses.
- Well-qualified and highly motivated academic staff involved in scholarship, publication, active in research and consultancy. Highly qualified and knowledgeable support staff.
- Accessible and fully utilized library provision with appropriate stocks.
- Responsiveness to IT developments, including video and satellite.

On the other hand, assessors have identified instances where some staff are under great pressure, with unacceptable demands being placed on them. Some facilities are under-utilized and other resources, such as teaching accommodation, need to take account of increasing student numbers. Reference has been made to weaknesses in the deployment of learning resources, including specialist equipment, IT and libraries.

Assessors' recommendations have shown strong similarities between subjects across the core aspects. However, most variations occur (not surprisingly) under the CDCO and LR aspects. For example, in some subjects staffing is an issue (eg applied social work) and in others accommodation is an issue (eg music). Also former PCFC institutions tend to fare less well than former UFC institutions under this aspect (QSC, 1996).

Sources of evidence for the LR aspect

Assessors review learning resources in the context of the subject aims and objectives they are designed to support. Any departmental literature outlining your learning resources strategy is likely to be scrutinized, such as the student handbook, minutes of a staff–student committee or a resources committee.

Observation of teaching and learning activities is a key source of evidence for the LR aspect. The observation form (Annex E, *Assessors' Handbook*, HEFCE, 1996a) makes specific reference to the effective use of accommodation, specialist equipment and materials, visual aids and IT. Observations will be supplemented by tours of central and departmental resources, including the library and computing services; laboratories; and students and staff (eg technical, administrative and secretarial). Assessors will make observations on their tours – are computer laboratories being used or are they empty? Are students queuing for print-outs or for access to a terminal? Do date stamps on books in the library indicate recent use?

Students could be asked questions about the nature of resources available (eg books, periodicals, computers, specialist equipment, study space and social areas), access to the resources (opening hours, availability of terminals) and training/support in their use. Students' views may open up new lines of enquiry for the assessors to follow. Assessors take student views seriously, but they do cross-reference them with other sources of evidence. In one assessment in which we were involved the team supported a department's claim that IT resources were sufficient, despite the complaints of some students. On checking for themselves, assessors found workstations available in IT laboratories every time they walked past them!

1. Strategy

(a) Learning resources strategy

An LR strategy should state clearly how your resources support student learning and should make explicit links to subject aims and objectives, the curriculum and TLA methods. Assessors should be able to understand the rationale for both the existence and use of all your resources. Provide evidence that decisions about purchasing, deploying, maintaining and updating resources are based on sound planning for the delivery of your programmes.

What mechanisms do you have for ensuring that students have the right resources and that they are fully utilized? The importance of a strategy is illustrated in assessors' comments in the subject overview report for French. 'Even where the resources are in place and their use is in line with published objectives, the take-up may remain low unless facilities are integrated within a clear teaching, learning and assessment strategy.' Similarly, for one-third of German providers, assessors noted a failure to exploit well-resourced language learning centres, largely due to the resources not being fully integrated within an overall learning strategy.

The LR strategy should outline how resource decisions are made. For example, if you have a new computing lab or a refurbished laboratory with specialist equipment, provide documentation to show the planning and consultation process, indicating the purpose of the resources. Consider how your resources are prioritized. Fieldwork is central to geology and it is clear from the subject overview report that most providers make this a priority in resource allocation, despite growth in student numbers. For French providers the increase in resource-based learning is often not accompanied by a coherent strategy for its use.

The Follett Report (1993) highlights the findings of a national survey conducted in 1992, identifying what students consider to be important factors contributing to quality. Out of a total of 111 criteria, three of the top five are related to the library and allied services. The study highlighted the importance of student access to the library, IT facilities and to the teaching staff. What mechanisms do you have for inviting student feedback on resources, for example staff–student committee or a student questionnaire, or for obtaining input from employers? If you have a resources committee is there a student representative from the library and computing services?

We explore the following issues in relation to a learning resources strategy:

(i)   match of learning resources to subject aims and objectives and to student profile;
(ii) learning resources to support curricula and TLA methods;
(iii) arrangements for maintaining, replacing and updating learning resources.

(i) Match of learning resources to subject aims and objectives and to student profile

You need to consider the specific objectives relevant to the LR aspect (probably all of them!) Some will have very obvious resource implications, such as staff specialisms, laboratories and equipment. In reality you will already have a fair idea of these, but perhaps you have not had to articulate so clearly the link between the resources and how they are used to meet your objectives. The range and nature of your resources may need to evolve due to changing curricula, financial constraints or student expectations. A resource strategy should include your policies on such issues. For example, in many engineering subjects the pace of technological change causes difficulties in the provision of equipment for practical classes. Some departments are turning to computer simulation to offset this.

The student profile may have a bearing on the learning resources, for example a wider variation in background is likely to demand a more flexible provision with a wider range of learning methods and materials – all with obvious resource implications. If your student numbers have been increasing, indicate how your resource strategy accommodates this. Examples include: more provision for private study; better short-loan procedures; scheduled sessions with IT facilities; the use of an optical mark reader to analyse assessment results and so on. Resource-based learning is a common response to increased student numbers and reduced contact time – and hopefully it may be introduced for sound educational reasons too! Whatever the reason, both staff and students require support for this mode of delivery. Staff need training in course design, the production of learning materials and integrating resource-based learning into a learning strategy. Students need to be equipped with the research and study skills.

Library provision for sociology was considered poorer for part-time students compared to those studying full time. This was because of the timing of the end of evening studies and the opening hours of learning resource centres which made access difficult. Examples of how such needs can be addressed include short-term loans for longer than one night, study packs with reading material for the course, or timetabling arrangements that enable student access to the resources at convenient times. Good practice includes the dedication of set textbook stock and separate loan arrangements for part-time students.

(ii) Learning resources to support curricula and TLA methods

From the CDCO aspect, assessors will have a good insight into your curriculum. As your peers they will know the sorts of resources needed to deliver the curriculum and will check that these are in place. Examples include: laboratories and equipment to support a practical-based curriculum; IT facilities and technical back-up to support IT integrated into the curriculum; effective library facilities to develop research skills. Each subject will demand its own set of special resources, for example, geology requires resources to support fieldwork; music to supply instruments and studios; computer studies to provide IT laboratories; and engineering to provide design studios. Rapid developments in your subject might demand regular review and updating of equipment.

The implications of course design for resources need to be accounted for in the TLA strategy. For example, a programme in which all students are taught the same thing at the same time (a lecture series with set reading material) means there will be a peak demand for the same reading material at the same time. In this case the library might have to introduce shorter loan periods and provide multiple copies of set texts, rather than a broad range. A more student-centred curriculum and delivery would create different demands on resources. If students were given more freedom in the choice of assignments or choosing specific topics, there would be less pressure on resources but resource needs would be more difficult to predict (Higgins *et al.*, 1996).

Resources should also be matched to your teaching and learning activities. For example, if you claim to support independent learning, ensure that you are providing students with sufficient resources, such as study space and IT equipment. You might set activities for students, such as field or laboratory work, which necessitate the use of dedicated learning resources. Resources should also be appropriate for your assessment activities. If, for example, you use a lot of multiple-choice tests for diagnostic purposes and for regular assessment of progress, it could be supported by the use of an optical mark reader to save time or marking, or the whole process could be electronic, using computer-aided assessment tools.

(iii) Arrangements for maintaining, replacing and updating learning resources

Your LR strategy should include arrangements for maintaining, replacing and updating resources. Provide resource maintenance and renewal records in the base room, with a summary of, say, the last two to three years. Central providers such as computing services might be asked for the rationale used in updating their provision. Are they aware of your LR strategy? Assessors will probably talk to technicians about this. Also include any forward planning in this regard, and show that you are alert to future trends. Many French providers were commended for high-quality language centres. In the best examples there is an on-going replacement programme that incorporates new technologies.

Consider your current resources and how they are maintained. If your resources are in a poor state of repair or out of date, you will need to ensure that the resources seen by assessors are sufficient to meet your aims and objectives. You don't need to have the latest equipment and technology, unless your subject aims and objectives are dependent upon them.

(b) Liaison with central services and departmental support staff

Here we consider the liaison between teaching staff and the staff who support their activities; this includes central services and departmental staff such as technicians and administrators. In sociology assessors recognize that closer links with central services have enabled a suitable strategy to be developed which looks at the full range of resources required. Effective liaison ensured that both central and subject developments were incorporated into new programmes. Assessors often comment that the best library provision benefits from effective liaison with subject specialists; the importance of effective cooperation between such staff is also stressed in the Follett Report (1993).

Higgins *et al.* (1996) believe that the distinction between academic and support staff, such as librarians, is becoming blurred. Libraries often provide training, for example information and study skills, note-taking and essay planning. However, Brewer (cited in Higgins *et al.*, 1996) found that support staff responsible for resources felt that they were under-utilized, despite having a lot to offer academic staff. Are library or computing services staff represented on your resource committee? Whatever the links between central services and the subject, assessors will be keen to know how effective they are from the students' point of view. Students probably will not know if you liaise formally with computing services but they will certainly have an opinion on IT resources. Are there enough and do students have access when they need them? Students invariably claim that they do not! The library and computing services can provide data for the framework section of your self-assessment. They can also contribute to the evaluative part of your self-assessment under the LR aspect, particularly if they have been consulted on your TLA strategy. Both services should be able to articulate their role in supporting the learning of your students.

By now the library and computing services will have been involved in a number of assessments and will probably have a prepared response. Examples of items in library resource packs include: information on facilities, induction documents, an information skills questionnaire and service reports. The pack might also include a list of the issues raised by assessors on visits to the library, such as spending on different areas, liaison with the department, procedures for ordering materials, time taken to return materials to shelves, discipline in the library, number of seats, accessibility of materials and cooperation with other libraries. Computing services might have similar material including student literature, statistics on student usage, training material and records of student feedback on services.

Do you inform your library and computing services about planned changes in curriculum content and developments in the provision so that they can develop their provision accordingly? For example, the library might need to buy more periodicals, develop customized learning packs, provide extra training or update reading lists. What special arrangements are required to accommodate the needs of your students? Computing services might need to provide more training, technical back-up or to improve access arrangements. Assessors of German identified good communication between library and subject staff and frequent reference was made to the integral role of subject librarians, who in the best cases are fully involved in course development and review. The latest HEFCE report on quality assessment (HEFCE, 1997b) commends the involvement of library and learning resources staff in course developments and reviews.

Consider the mechanisms for liaising with the technical and administrative staff in your department. Are technical staff kept up to date with specialist equipment and how students are required to use it? Invite technical and administrative staff to provide feedback regarding students' use of resources. What difficulties do students experience and how are they addressed on a day-to-day basis?

2. Library resources

(c) Availability and accessibility to all students

Assessors will be keen to determine if students have access to the resources they need, when they need them. They may look at loan periods, availability of duplicate copies, library opening hours (in and out of term), and practical access for all students including part-time, disabled and distance learners.

Many students today are short of money. Do you have any arrangements to support students who cannot afford to buy books, for example, short-loan copies or a departmental library? Assessors noted French providers who had alleviated the problem of insufficient copies of commonly used texts through short-loan schemes, study packs and CD-ROMs. Be aware of the study patterns of your students. Are they all fighting for the same book at the same time and, if so, is this because of poor planning by students or the clustering of assessment? If it is the latter, review curriculum design and consequent workload to avoid peak demand for the same resource at the same time.

(d) Induction and ongoing user support

Does the library provide induction to its facilities and is it customized to the needs of your students? More to the point, what proportion of your students attend? Outline the type of induction the library provides for students including all types of training and ongoing support offered. Training may include courses on time management or the use of self-study materials. In linguistics, librarians and staff from other learning resource services provide training in library research skills and computer skills to support project and dissertation work. Include any induction and support materials in the base room.

(e) Books, periodical stocks, learning packs and study spaces

HEFCE reports (1995e, 1997b) have identified some difficulties in the provision of appropriate resources to support the curriculum, particularly in former PCFC institutions. Assessors note the considerable pressure on resources in sociology as a result of large student numbers; in many cases this has been compensated by the production of course materials. Linguistics assessors recognize the difficulty of balancing the requirement for depth and breadth of the subject, also the demand for multiple copies of frequently used textbooks; all this with limited resources.

Students need a quiet place to study, particularly if you encourage independent study. When describing the study places available for students, consider the accessibility of the study space. Is it available after 5pm or out of term? If resource-based learning forms a key part of your provision, assessors are likely to scrutinize the materials used. Of course this would form a key part of the assessment for the Open University, for example.

3. Equipment and IT

(f) Availability and accessibility, including arrangements for students to work independently

If students complain about access to equipment or IT facilities, is there any way to alleviate the problem? It is likely that there will be peaks and troughs of usage. Can the demand be spread out rather than clustered? Is student usage monitored? Do students make use of out-of-hours access if it is available? Assessors are likely to check this themselves if access is considered to be an issue.

Arrangements for independent learning should be outlined in the subject TLA strategy. Indicate how it is integrated into the entire programme, outline the support required for students and staff and identify the implications for learning resources. Assessors' comments on facilities for independent learning are mixed. However, reference to a lack of strategy for independent or resource-based learning is quite common. Assessors of French suggest that expectations regarding independent learning should be explicitly defined for students and their understanding and progress must be checked.

(g) General and specialist equipment

If your students use a lot of technology, for example, specialist equipment, e-mail, video-conferencing or CD-ROM, make sure that you document your strategy for incorporating technology into your teaching. Many IT facilities are used by language providers. These include: satellite television, multimedia resource centres, CD-ROM, e-mail, World Wide Web, computerized library catalogues and computer-assisted language learning (CALL). Assessors of French recognize that specialist IT provision generally meets the requirements of curricula, but there may be a need for improvement and clearer strategies for its use if it is to cater for new developments. Similarly, assessors of German note that the majority of providers do not have an obvious strategy for embedding IT in the curriculum despite subject-specific and transferable skills being effectively incorporated.

Information technology might be a key part of your curriculum, in which case assessors will need to establish if your IT resources are up to scratch and enable objectives to be met. The high quality of IT facilities is recognized as a significant strength for the majority of linguistic providers, for example PC workstations, some multimedia facilities, networked computers and e-mail. There are well-equipped specialist facilities including purpose-built laboratories with facilities for experimental work in computational linguistics, interactive video and phonetic recording and analysis. However, recent increases in student numbers are making it difficult to sustain adequate IT provision.

Assessors highlight a number of issues relating to IT – a lack of IT policy, insufficient attention given to the development of IT skills, and the potential of IT not always being realized. For sociology, assessors found that staff who have been trained in IT recognize the opportunities technology can bring. However, there are examples where such resources are not used and assessors identified the need for further staff development in order that facilities are employed to the full benefit by students. If students use equipment and IT resources in laboratory exercises and project work, for example, indicate the training and support they have in use of the equipment and the technical back-up. Also outline how you ensure that such equipment is kept up to date.

(h) Learning materials, for example TLTP

This issue relates as much to paper-based materials as technology-based learning materials. Materials may include CAL packages, material on the Web, e-mail or specially designed paper-based packages to cover certain parts of the curriculum. HEFCE is concerned to evaluate the effectiveness of Teaching and Learning Technology Programme (TLTP) materials, so if you are part of such a project refer to it in your self-assessment and provide evidence in the base room of its progress in supporting learning. Assessors might even observe a session with students using the materials.

(i) Induction and ongoing user support

Where possible provide documentation on induction and support for the use of equipment and IT resources. Assessors of Russian and Eastern European languages and studies commend the excellent range of IT facilities and the integration of IT into teaching, but in some cases the induction into and use of IT facilities is not well integrated into the curriculum. Similarly, assessors of sociology believe a considerable improvement can be made in the development and application of IT skills. Assessors of Italian commented on institutions in which students need further training to make use of IT resources, including computer-assisted language learning (CALL).

Assessors have ample opportunity to talk to departmental computer officers and technicians and they may visit computing services. Who provides training and support? In particular, consider the support available for the use of specialist equipment. Are students confident in using the equipment or do they need supervision?

4. Teaching and social accommodation

(j) Suitability of teaching, social, dining and recreational accommodation

Accommodation for teaching and learning could include lecture halls, tutorial rooms, studios, laboratories and learning resource rooms. Some subjects such as music or the performing arts rely on purpose-built accommodation. Similarly assessors recognize that the laboratories needed to teach engineering and science subjects, which are expensive to establish and maintain.

Assessors comment on the suitability of rooms for learning, for example room size, acoustics, lighting and temperature. For some music providers assessors found difficulties with sound interference between rooms and pressure on the availability of practice rooms. A number of chemical engineering providers suffer from extraneous noise that interferes with the teaching process, particularly for institutions on urban campuses. However, assessors do commend the imaginative efforts of teachers in making the most of less than ideal accommodation. In sociology, assessors note that some of the more interesting teaching took place in some of the less promising accommodation. Consider the learning resources available in the rooms themselves. One left-handed assessor was not impressed with chairs in a lecture hall which had pad rests on the right-hand side only. Make sure that assessors are able to see all your facilities and accommodation – arrange a tour for them if necessary.

Social, dining and recreational accommodation are important to the educational experience, providing the 'atmosphere' of the learning environment

– the meeting places where academic matters are discussed (such as cribbing coursework solutions). They also play an important role in enhancing staff–student and student–student interaction. Assessors of German identified good examples of common rooms and a range of integrated accommodation that creates a supportive sense of subject identity. It is easy to be cynical about these things ('the lavatories were painted', UCML, 1996), but they do give an impression of how much the department cares about the students.

Often, much is made of social and recreational facilities in prospectuses and other institutional and departmental publicity. Do they live up to the glossy description? Assessors have found in some cases that there is an excessive strain on physical resources, which is often exacerbated by recent increases in student numbers. In some cases this has led to deficiencies related to health and safety, for example, students not using goggles in laboratory classes. Understandably such deficiencies will be penalized, as will the fact that it has been left to the assessors to uncover them.

5. Technical and administrative support

(k) Technical and administrative support for utilization of learning resources

This is a crucial area, particularly in practical courses. Consider the technical and administrative support for use of learning resources at departmental and institutional level. The amount of support is likely to be dependent on the nature of your provision and the specialist equipment, laboratory-based provision and use of learning resource materials. Some subjects will demand a high level of technical support. For example, assessors identified the need for well-qualified audio technicians to support the rapid growth of technology courses and electronic music facilities in music.

If technical and administrative staff play a key role in supporting learning, consider what training they receive to enable their role. Do you encourage and support your technical and administrative staff to study for further qualifications?

Chapter 9

Quality assurance and enhancement

This chapter covers issues for quality assurance and enhancement (QAE).

1. Quality assurance and enhancement strategy

(a) documented strategy for QAE
(b) provision assured by the strategy.

2. Evaluating the provision

(c) evaluation methods used
(d) validity and reliability of evaluation methods.

3. Developing the provision

(e) effective infrastructure for taking action
(f) action taken in response to evaluation outcomes.

4. Procedural guidelines and record keeping

(g) procedural documentation
(h) record keeping
(i) allocation of responsibilities
(j) scheduling.

Introduction

A comment on the issues

The key issues we have given for this aspect do not correspond to the assessors' *aide-mémoire*. As we explain below, we think that the *aide-mémoire* can be improved as a tool for assessing quality assurance and enhancement (QAE) mechanisms, and have proposed an alternative based on the following principles.

A QAE strategy defines what is evaluated, the evaluation methods used, how the developmental response will be made and how the whole process will be implemented. The strategy consists of an **evaluation phase**, in which an area of provision is *assessed* and the results *analysed*. The outcomes of this phase form the input to a **development phase** in which *advice* is given on *action* to be taken, possibly with *assistance*. For each of the five processes – assess, analyse, advise, act and assist – documented procedural guidelines are required on *how* it is implemented, *who* will do it and *when* it will be done. Effective *records* of the outcomes are also maintained.

These principles are designed to apply to any QAE procedure at any level, from institutional down to individual teaching and learning session. We enlarge on these later, but for now note how these principles are reflected in the key issues. Note also that we favour 'evaluation and development' over 'assurance and enhancement'. The former is more supportive and formative.

The evolution of QAE mechanisms in HEIs

The QAE aspect considers all mechanisms for assuring and enhancing the quality of the entire educational provision. For objectives at every level – programme, course, session – the question may be asked, 'How do you know you are achieving them?' The HEQC quality audit process looks at whether the mechanisms are in place to provide answers to this question. Quality assessment looks at your institution's outcomes in the audit exercise and the responses made to HEQC recommendations. The QAE aspect then considers how you respond to the outcomes of your quality assurance mechanisms, in order to improve your provision. This includes staff development, for example. As we discuss below, the QAE aspect has attracted much comment from assessors. Certainly this is one of the aspects that requires the closest attention by HEIs. The same can be said of further education, in which a lower percentage of colleges gained the highest grade in quality assurance than in any other aspect (FEDA, 1995).

Why, then, is this aspect such a problem? The clue lies in the statistics that show that the former PCFC-funded institutions, which had the benefit of CNAA monitoring, tended to do better in QAE. The fact is that HEIs, particularly the 'older' ones, have never had the detailed scrutiny of every aspect of their educational provision to which they are now subject. They have never been expected to assure or enhance their provision in such a way. They have always had some degree of quality assurance, through validation and review mechanisms for courses and programmes, and the external examiner system. However, these normally focused on curriculum content or student assessment. Their main concern is outcome rather than process. Quality assessment, on the other hand, scrutinizes all provision – process and outcome – and only in recent years have institutions begun to respond with such things as student questionnaires and sometimes classroom observation. As the subject overview reports for the 1995–96 round attest, this response has often been reactive and ad hoc, resulting in piecemeal, half-hearted QAE systems short on rigour, structure and documentation.

The HEFCE *aide-mémoire* for the QAE aspect

We believe that the quality assessment documentation, such as the key features and the *aide-mémoire* for the QAE aspect (HEFCE, 1996a), reflect the ad hoc development of QAE systems referred to above. For example, the HEFCE *aide-mémoire* is methodology led. It encourages the user to think of student questionnaires, internal validation, external examiners, and so on, and then to consider what these methods tell us about the provision. The reverse should be the case: think about what it is that you want to assure or evaluate, consider the methods that will enable you to do it and then make a selection to suit your purposes. This ensures that you cover all that you want to, whereas starting from the methods end you cannot be sure that you have not left something out. Assessors in the 1995–96 round frequently called attention to areas of provision that were not evaluated by some providers, such as periods abroad, library and learning resources, and to a lack of systematic monitoring of the achievement of aims and objectives.

In general, the *aide-mémoire* is not systematic in its treatment of the key elements of any effective QAE system, ie: purpose, focus, evaluation method, 'closing the loop', documentation, lines of responsibility, timeliness, and validity and reliability of evaluation methods. For example, the important requirement for complete and accurate documentation is not explicit; the importance of 'closing the loop' on all evaluative processes is tucked away in 'action as appropriate' on a selection of methods. The need for specific organizational infrastructure in which every stage in the QAE process is someone's specific responsibility, is only implicit and not spelt out. There is no obvious place for the *focus* of evaluation, ie what it is that you evaluate.

Key issues for the QAE aspect

Our QAE issues have a different structure to the HEFCE *aide-mémoire*. The principles underlying the issues can be illustrated by a simple example. The classroom delivery of Dr X can be *assessed* by student questionnaire and peer observation, and the results *analysed* to produce an **evaluation** of the quality of delivery. The outcomes can be considered by a teaching **development** committee, which *advises* that Dr X takes *action* to disseminate the good practice observed through workshops, *assisted* by staff development.

Broadly, then, our issues consider:

1. the *QAE strategy* and what is covered by it
2. *evaluating the provision* by valid and reliable means
3. *developing the provision* in response to the outcomes
4. appropriate *procedural guidelines and recording keeping.*

The point of focusing on the key generic processes assess, analyse, advise, act and assist (the '5As'), is that by ensuring that each is properly implemented we can design a rigorous, comprehensive QAE system to suit a provider's local needs. This systematic procedural implementation also avoids common deficiencies in QAE mechanisms: the gathering of more data than can be processed; the absence of a robust structure to effect action; failure to close the loop; lack of identified responsibility; and absence of support and help.

Some readers might prefer to use the HEFCE *aide-mémoire* – after all, that is the 'exam paper'! However, we believe that our set of issues is more systematic, and is easily mapped onto the *aide-mémoire* if desired. The underlying principles define a procedure by which you can design your own QAE strategy and mechanisms to suit your needs.

What the assessors say about the QAE aspect

For the 272 providers assessed in the 1995–96 round 16 per cent received a grade 2 (by far the highest proportion of 2s awarded for any aspect), half received a grade 3, and 34 per cent of providers were awarded 4s. The QAE aspect produced the lowest overall average grade. The former PCFC sector institutions received a higher average grade and a higher proportion of grade 4s in the QAE aspect than the former UFC institutions. This probably reflects their experience of CNAA.

Under the QAE aspect the assessors identified the following broad characteristics of high quality education.

- Clear and consistent aims and objectives that are well understood by staff and students and are achieved.

- Systematic and effective monitoring of achievement of aims and objectives.
- Evaluative, analytical self-assessment.
- Staff development mechanisms that are focused on quality enhancement.
- Monitoring of teaching methods and the student learning experience.
- Effective collection and dissemination of student feedback and external opinion.
- High levels of student satisfaction.
- Speedy response to identified issues.
- Sharing of good teaching and learning practice.
- Effective induction arrangements for new staff of all categories.
- Systematic approach to identifying the training needs of all staff.
- Expertise in teaching as a criterion for staff promotion and career development. (HEFCE, 1997b)

On the negative side, assessors still see many examples of the main problems with HEI quality procedures – over-reliance on informal mechanisms and ineffectual 'closing the loop' in acting on issues identified. They point to the need for improved take-up of staff development, particularly by more experienced staff. The increasing reliance on the use of postgraduate assistants and part-time teachers is also producing a demand for support for such staff.

Sources of evidence for the QAE aspect

Evidence for the QAE aspect might be scattered throughout a number of departmental and institutional documents, or might not be documented at all. Institutional literature on its quality procedures should set the context at institutional level, but assessors will also need to know how this links with your own departmental procedures. This can be described in your QAE strategy document.

The documentation that assessors will consult includes departmental records, external examiners' reports, internal review committee minutes and reports, accreditation documentation and the HEQC audit report. The last will be of particular interest to them and they will look for evidence that you have acted on the outcomes. It would be useful, for the assessors' reference, to have a file of procedural guidelines and records kept on all evaluation methods used and any developmental activities undertaken. The raw data, such as completed student questionnaires, can be available should assessors want to dig deeper. It might be useful to have some case studies of the ways in which your QAE procedures have resulted in improvement in recent years; for example, outcomes and action on student feedback or external examiners' comments.

Assessors will ask students about quality assurance and enhancement in your subject. For the QAE aspect, the assessors' agenda items for the meeting with students are:

- ways in which students' views are sought
- representation on course/departmental committees
- the degree to which students' views are influential
- students' contribution to the self-assessment. (HEFCE, 1996a)

1. Quality assurance and enhancement strategy

(a) Documented strategy for QAE

If you want to do well in this aspect a clear documented strategy for QAE is highly desirable. This should include a statement of the purpose of QAE; the methods used to assess each aspect of the provision; how the outcomes are analysed; how the results are turned into developmental activities; how the impact on the provision is monitored; and scheduling and resourcing. It is important that the strategy is understood and 'owned' by the stakeholders concerned, including staff and students. It should, in principle, be possible for assessors to see from the strategy how you assure and enhance every aspect of your provision. They can then follow through a few examples to test its effectiveness.

Specific areas that a QAE strategy at subject level might include are:

- links with institutional QAE mechanisms and external processes such as quality assessment
- induction and appraisal
- staff development policy, including identification of training needs
- promotion and reward for teaching
- ownership by staff and students.

While assessors have noted an over-reliance on informal systems, the strategy and mechanisms should not be cumbersome or over-complicated, as this can be self-defeating.

A procedure for designing QAE strategies

The ad hoc evolution of quality methodology in higher education does not help providers in developing a strategy for QAE, and the fragments of existing procedures already in place sometimes confuse matters. We describe below a simple procedure by which you can design your own strategy for dealing with QAE, tailored to your local needs. The procedure is applicable to any evaluation and development activity, at any level, but here we are focusing on the subject level. It is essentially a series of systematic steps by which a selection of evaluation methods is made to suit the focus(es) of evaluation, and an infrastructure is set up to turn the outcomes of evaluation into developmental responses – ie who does what, when.

We believe it is important that providers design their own strategy, to meet their own local needs, rather than trying to adopt an off-the-peg version. In the subject overview reports for Italian, chemical engineering and sociology assessors commented that in some institutions staff had not really bought into the QAE mechanisms, for various reasons. For example, in some chemical engineering provision 'academic staff are by no means convinced of the value of comprehensive monitoring, review and evaluation procedures in assessing and enhancing quality. Such a lack of conviction was manifested in the generally mediocre self-assessment documents.' A quality system that does not have strong support from those involved is unlikely to be very effective, and support is more likely to be forthcoming if they have had a hand in designing the system.

To provide the required flexibility and portability the procedure focuses on the implementation of the 5As. For each of these processes, you have to describe and document how it will be done, who will do it, when it will be done, and how it will be resourced (Cox and Ingleby, 1997).

The *evaluation phase* is implemented by an evaluation scheme designed by working systematically through the following six steps.

1. Define the purpose(s) of the evaluation – *why* you are evaluating.
2. Define the focus(es) of the evaluation – *what* it is that you are evaluating.
3. Consider the different methods of evaluation available, ensuring that each is a valid and reliable tool.
4. Identify a *range of evaluation methods* that may contribute to the evaluation of each focus defined in step 2.
5. Select a suitable number of *independent evaluation methods* for each focus.
6. Decide on the *scheduling* of the evaluation scheme – how often, what, when, etc.

For example, you might decide to evaluate the quality of your pastoral support for students (what) as part of a review of the SSG aspect in readiness for quality assessment (why) in, say, 18 months' time. This could be done by student questionnaire, interviewing students and staff, consulting student records, or talking to central student support services (range of methods). You may choose to interview staff, consult central services and gather student feedback by a questionnaire (selection), making sure that the information you obtain is valid and reliable. Since you want to implement any improvements well before the assessors descend, you might plan to complete the evaluation within three months, which will give you 15 months to implement, monitor and refine the new system (schedule).

The *developmental phase* is implemented by establishing an organizational infrastructure in which someone will *advise* on developmental responses, someone will act to implement the responses and others might provide *assistance*. For each of these processes you need to decide how it will be done, assign responsibilities and plan a schedule.

Continuing the example of pastoral support, the outcomes of the evaluation process might be submitted to a group set up to prepare for quality assessment. They would consider the implications in the context of the overall preparation. The evaluation outcomes might indicate that this is a weak area of provision, lacking structure, clear responsibilities and consistent guidelines. The group might then advise that a small departmental working group be set up to design a code of practice, with associated documentation, within a timescale of two months. The working group might seek assistance from the central support services and possibly from a department which has been recently commended by assessors for its pastoral support of students. A member of the working group might be designated to implement and monitor the code of practice and report back to the quality assessment group once a term.

There are many approaches to developing quality assurance and enhancement strategies and procedures. Many of these, such as Total Quality Management and ISO9000, have commercial or industrial origins that might not be wholly appropriate for educational environments. Interesting models designed for higher education include the institutional-level Quality Improvement in Learning and Teaching (QILT) scheme (Laycock, 1996) and the departmental-level Quality Management Framework prepared for the Engineering Professors' Council (Burge *et al.*, 1996) and supported by HEFCE, HEQC, and engineering PSBs. We emphasize, however, that these are not alternatives to the procedure we are describing, but rather particular examples of what can be designed using the procedure we have described. Our procedure is a means of designing QAE strategies and mechanisms to suit any provision at any level.

(b) Provision assured by the strategy

It would be wise these days to ensure that *all* aspects of your provision are evaluated and continually improved. Assessors have noted that even traditionally strong areas such as programme and course design review are not always dealt with rigorously. When considering the focus of evaluation you might start at a coarse level corresponding to a general issue such as the mechanisms for giving feedback on students' work. You might then dig deeper by *progressive focusing*, evaluating things at a more detailed level, such as the quality of the feedback given by individual staff. The key point is to decide exactly what it is that you want to evaluate.

Assessors consider equal opportunities under the QAE aspect. HEFCE policy on equal opportunities can be found in the *Assessors' Handbook*. Assessors will look for evidence that you operate an equal opportunities policy and monitor its effectiveness. This may impact on access, accommodation, the curriculum and so on. As well as explicit equal opportunities violations, there could be some implicit biases. For example, in an assessment of one law department it was found that the bulk of women went into family law while the more prestigious courses such as company law were the preserve of the male students. The department had not considered the reasons for this, or whether it was a reasonable situation.

2. Evaluating the provision

(c) Evaluation methods used

The evaluation methods used will be the means by which data are extracted from various sources (see Chapter 2), for example, obtaining feedback from students by questionnaire. Rather than attempt to give full commentary of the many available evaluation methods (Cox, 1994; Gibbs *et al.*, 1989; O'Neil and Pennington, 1992; Partington, 1993; Ramsden and Dodds, 1989) we concentrate on the main methods encountered by assessors during the 1995–96 round:

- institutional mechanisms such as programme review and validation committees
- HEQC audit
- external examiners' reports
- student feedback
- staff appraisal
- peer observation and review
- self-assessment document
- employers and professional bodies
- management information systems.

Institutional mechanisms

Assessors are interested in institutional mechanisms to assure and enhance quality on an institution-wide basis; for example, review and validation committees, faculty boards, or quality committees. These will have been reviewed under audit and the assessors will be interested to see what use has been made of the audit report in enhancing the quality for the subject provision. They will also want to know how the provider or departmental-level mechanisms relate to the institutional mechanisms. For example, student feedback and external examiners' reports might say that a new course or a significant modification to an established course is required. This could be considered, designed and proposed by a departmental curriculum committee and ratified by a full departmental meeting. The outcome could be submitted to Faculty Board, from there to a first degrees validating committee and then to Senate for final approval. The assessors will certainly expect to see a clearly documented trail through this process, with records of meetings outlining progress. This is exactly the sort of evidence they will be looking for as proof that your quality assurance and enhancement mechanisms are working.

HEQC audit report

The HEQC quality audit report provides recommendations mainly at an institutional level on a whole range of matters, most of which have implications for departmental provision. It is essential to ensure at first that everyone is effectively informed about the outcomes of audit. We have heard of cases where the person putting the self-assessment together was unaware of the existence of the audit report, let alone informed about its content or implications for provision. As well as the institutional audit reports, two excellent sources of information and good practice are the HEQC publications *Learning from Audit* (HEQC, 1994b, 1996b).

External examiners' reports

A wide variability in the operation of the external examiner system has emerged from quality audit (HEQC, 1997). If they are adequately rewarded, external examiners can often provide far more information on your provision than you might realize. Refer to the aspect issues raised in previous chapters – are there areas on which your external examiner could comment?

Traditionally, the external examiner's role is to ensure that:

- degrees awarded in similar subjects are comparable in standard across higher education institutions; and
- students are dealt with fairly in the assessment and classification system in a given institution.

While HEFCE quality assessment does not concern itself with standards, assessors do consider external examiners' reports and how they are acted on. Assessors might ask for briefing papers or guidelines issued to external examiners, as well as their completed reports.

The Quality Support Centre of the Open University was commissioned by the HEQC to look into the present effectiveness and future of the external examiner system from the point of view of HEIs and in relation to the system's acknowledged central purposes. The outcome was published as a Quality Support Centre report (HEQC, 1997; QSC, 1995).

The report emphasized the continuing importance of the external examiner system, particularly in the monitoring of the fairness of assessment and examination procedures. However, it perceived a growing need for change, arising from such issues as modularization, semesterization and increased student numbers. Remuneration was also highlighted as a critical issue, with too much reliance on goodwill. The absence of an overall national standard for higher education makes the external examiners' role as the 'guardians of standards' increasingly difficult to fulfil; however, the *Graduate Standards Programme* (HEQC, 1996a) should help in this respect. The implications of diversity are also complicating the role of the external examiner.

The report emphasized the need for briefing, induction and training of external examiners. External examiners are seen as key in strengthening internal quality control and assurance. The report identified strong support for the recognition of external examining as a legitimate, expected, costed part of the normal duties of academic staff. A national register of people available for external examining is also strongly supported. The nature, procedures and impact of external quality scrutiny in general need to be borne in mind when considering the future operation of the external examiner system. This includes the interests of validating and validated institutions. (For more on the external examiner system, see Partington *et al.*, 1993.)

Student feedback

Learning from Audit 1 (HEQC, 1994b) noted a wide variety of student feedback mechanisms, for example:

- formal representation on school and divisional boards and on academic boards/senates and sub-committees;
- student membership/representation on formal panels for programme approval and review;
- student membership of staff–student liaison committees;
- student involvement in evaluation sessions;
- suggestion boxes;
- surveys of past graduates;
- fax and phone helplines for students on distance learning programmes;
- student questionnaires;
- student involvement in preparing feedback sessions as part of an annual monitoring process.

The two most common methods of student feedback are questionnaires and staff–student committees.

Student questionnaires are best kept short and simple. Do not overload the students and avoid collecting superfluous data or more data than you can handle. To improve validity make your questions focused and specific and be sure to pilot them. Students must understand what the questions mean, what feedback you require and what you will do about the outcomes. Some departments involve students in the design of questionnaires. Student questionnaires could be based on items of the assessors' *aide-mémoire* or the agenda for meetings with students. You could use student questionnaires as an initial means of identifying problems that may then be discussed in detail at a staff–student meeting.

It is best to analyse the outcomes of questionnaires quickly and concentrate on a limited number of key concerns, summarizing the outcomes for dissemination and keeping students informed at each stage. Tell students how they are benefiting from feedback from previous students. Consolidate the lessons learned into the provision and monitor the outcome, ensuring that problems do not repeat themselves.

Rather than a student questionnaire you could select a set of issues as the basis of a structured interview with a group of students, using the nominal group technique (Gibbs *et al.*, 1989). In this case you don't have to worry about return rates, you can clarify misunderstandings, monitor students' reactions and obtain immediate results. There is no paperwork to wade through, just a succinct summary of the main points that emerge.

Staff–student liaison committees came in for particular attention in *Learning from Audit* reports (HEQC 1994b, 1996b). Some of the difficulties noted in audit reports associated with this form of feedback were:

- a lack of a formal constitution or remit for the staff–student committee;
- agenda not being circulated in good time before meetings or discussion documents not being distributed in advance to help representatives elicit student opinion;
- students being unaware of opportunities to bring agenda items to committees and being uncertain of the authority of certain committees;
- minutes not containing clear indications for agreed actions or responsibilities for implementation;
- meetings dominated by staff so that the students felt unable to speak;
- no link with other feedback processes (such as results of questionnaires);
- long delays in processing criticisms and requests so that those raising the issues did not profit from the solutions;
- recurring, unresolved problems reappearing and some students expressing disillusionment as to the impact of their involvement on subsequent action;
- variations in response to concerns raised across the university, which may damage the credibility of the system as a whole.

The role of such committees should be outlined in the QAE strategy. Many of the above criticisms could be easily addressed by having a formal infrastructure in which it is clear who is responsible for what, with documented procedural guidelines and a schedule known to all involved. Students can also benefit from training in their role as representatives, and this can be supported by the Students' Guild.

Staff appraisal

Assessors are not allowed to see confidential appraisal reports and it is often difficult for them to determine whether or not appraisal has had a positive impact on teaching and learning. They might question staff to get their views on this and they will probably be interested in appraisal mechanisms. Despite their confidentiality, it is usually possible to collate some of the outcomes of appraisal and use them to devise a coherent planned response, through staff consultation. If you have an effective appraisal system, outline the appraisal policy, provide relevant documentation and outline developments that have been made as a result. If you don't have an appraisal system, indicate what other means you have for reviewing teaching skills.

Peer observation and review

Assessors regard this mechanism as highly important in assuring quality and enhancing it by dissemination of good practice. They have observed many embryonic schemes of this kind and the quality assessment and subject overview reports for 1995–96 contain numerous examples of good practice. They are particularly impressed by examples in which the staff are trained for the purpose. We have discussed peer evaluation in Chapters 2 and 5. Be sure that you have appropriate procedural documentation on your peer review system available for inspection during the visit. Completed anonymous observation sheets with audit trails would also be of value to the assessors.

The use of the self-assessment in the QAE aspect

Preparation of the self-assessment is itself a process of evaluating every aspect of your provision and producing evidence to support your evaluation. In fact, in the further education quality assessment system this is the precise function of the self-assessment: it is regarded as a review mechanism of your provision to be annually updated. The use of the self-assessment in this way is assessed under the QAE aspect. Assessors will regard an accurate and rigorous self-assessment as evidence of a healthy self-critical ethos within the department.

In the 1995–96 round assessors found much to commend in self-assessments. For example, assessors in sociology were able to report active student involvement in the production of some self-assessments. They also found a number of self-assessments that were deficient in one respect or another, for example, lack of self-criticism and evaluation, significant omissions, inadequate statistical evidence particularly in respect of student progression, and lack of exemplars to support claims.

The assessors will expect to see action taken on the weaknesses identified in the self-assessment and dissemination of the strengths. In the issues/evidence grid described in Chapter 2 we illustrated how you can examine each issue and identify, with evidence, your strengths and weaknesses. By addressing these and informing the assessors how you have done so, you will provide systematic evidence for this issue.

Employers and professional bodies where appropriate

Feedback from employers can be obtained by representation on internal committees, where they can offer input to the curriculum in terms of currency and employment skills, for example. Is the feedback obtained from employers informed; are they sufficiently familiar with your provision? Feedback can also be obtained during sandwich placements, through employers' reports on the progress of placement students. Where appropriate, assessors might ask to meet a group of employers for discussion about your provision. As well as input to curriculum development, assessors may ask about their input to quality mechanisms, if any.

Where relevant, assessors review the accreditation documents of professional bodies. This is important for the CDCO and QAE aspects in particular. You might even decide to have a joint quality assessment and accreditation visit. The QAAHE is currently seeking to work more closely with PSBs, and HEFCE outlines different collaborative models in Circular 3/97 (HEFCE, 1997a).

Management information systems

Assessors identify the need for a significant number of providers to improve their management information systems, including the quality of the statistics submitted, particularly on student progression. In sociology for example:

> 'A number of providers encountered difficulty in supplying suitable and current information on the students on the courses. This was not helped by the development of modular provision where responsibility for monitoring progression was unclear.' (HEFCE, 1996f)

We have discussed such matters under the SPA aspect, which highlights the problem in quality assessment that the same points may come up under different aspects. Make sure that you are not penalized twice for the same underlying problem.

(d) Validity and reliability of evaluation methods

Many evaluation methods are rather blunt instruments and it is doubtful that assessors expect a high degree of rigour in their use. A simple rule of thumb is that if you do not have a fair degree of confidence that a tool does what you want it to, most of the time, it is not worth the trouble of using it. So it is with evaluation methods – we want to feel some confidence in what we get out of them. Validity can be improved by focusing enquiry on precise issues, and ensuring that whoever is providing the feedback is clear about your requirements. Similarly, you want to be sure that your data are reliable. For example, ensure that your student representatives on staff–student committees are in fact representative, and are trained in how to represent their fellow students most effectively. It is important to be fairly sure about the outcomes of all the methods that you use. Increasing the reliability of outcomes requires extra work, such as being proactive in setting the agenda for staff–student meetings, eliciting feedback on the key concerns, and following up responses with wider ranging surveys of the student body. Triangulation of feedback on the same issues from different sources also improves reliability.

In a recent quality assessment report of a department which obtained a profile of six grade 4s, reference was made to 'verbal' feedback as a useful form of evidence. This is exactly the sort of informal evidence on which most of us have relied up until now, and which some might think is hardly valid or reliable. However, assessors do appear to recognize it as an acceptable mechanism; if you mention informal feedback in the self-assessment, students will be asked about it. Indeed, *Learning from Audit* (HEQC, 1994b) notes the value of informal feedback, particularly in small departments, provided appropriate care is taken with confidentiality. Of course, such mechanisms are insufficient on their own and should be part of more formalized procedures.

Assessors have made many comments relating to the lack of rigour in student feedback, particularly by questionnaires. They have found problems with focus, effectiveness, consistency, depth of questioning, inadequate analysis and poor returns. Most providers have some improvements to make in the area of student feedback. Ensure reliability by completion under controlled conditions, say in class, by setting a high response rate (above 60 per cent) and by cross-reference with other sources of feedback to ensure feedback is not from one source that may be biased. Often the form and analysis of student questionnaires varies greatly from one department to another, and at institutional level audit teams have suggested the need for a greater degree of uniformity, or consistency. A useful compromise is to have a core set of questions common to every department, with additional menu questions for specific departments.

As mentioned previously, assessors have also noted the need for training student representatives and committee members, and staff involved in peer observation. Training should help to improve the validity and reliability of the methods. It is interesting to note that the Joint Planning Group report (1996) frequently uses the terms 'validity' and 'reliability' in reference to quality assurance mechanisms, so perhaps we are in for a more rigorous approach from the new QAAHE.

3. Developing the provision

(e) Effective infrastructure for taking action

To talk of a formal infrastructure can seem almost managerial. However, many of the shortcomings of quality mechanisms in higher education arise precisely because little attention is paid to systematic, organized, well staffed and resourced infrastructures for implementing them. By effective infrastructure we mean an appropriately resourced and staffed organization, in which people with designated responsibilities are charged with turning the outcomes of systematic evaluation into developmental responses; overseeing their implementation; and monitoring their impact on the provision. At subject level, for example, this could be a teaching committee that receives the results of various evaluation methods and decides on an appropriate response. This might include referral of a problem to staff development for advice or dissemination of identified good practice. Thus, having assessed and analysed an aspect of the provision, somebody is responsible for advising and acting on the outcomes, possibly with assistance from someone else. This may be applied at all levels, from the whole institution down to classroom teaching, where a pair of critical friends might be all there is to the 'infrastructure'.

Returning to our procedure for designing QAE strategies (pages 132–5), the infrastructure for implementing the developmental phase could be designed by mapping the *advise, act* and *assist* processes onto your local context. You will have to decide how to implement each process for your particular purposes, select or identify the required personnel, and arrange for appropriate scheduling and documentation.

It is particularly important that the roles of staff are identified at every stage of a quality assurance and enhancement process in a *durable* manner – ie the duties, tenure and position of each post are documented independent of the post-holder. Too often a particular stage relies informally on the energy and commitment of one individual, and if they leave the whole process falls apart. Assessors will expect such matters to be clear in your QAE strategy, and they should be able to locate and quiz staff with specific responsibilities. Time and again assessors have criticized providers for failure or tardiness in taking action on issues raised, particularly in response to audit, student feedback and external examiners' comments. The lack of a formal, permanent and embedded infrastructure also leaves staff and students unsure about mechanisms and their effectiveness. Assessors point to poor communication links, again a consequence of a weak infrastructure.

Are 'quality officers' given appropriate job titles and specifications? Is the work required of such staff recognized in the allocation of workload? For example, a figure of 20 per cent of teaching time is not an unreasonable allocation for evaluation and development of teaching: this is a significant workload. Some of it will be spread amongst all staff, but various generic aspects, such as design of student questionnaires, could be done by one person. Often, such work is regarded as 'one more job for the senior tutor', which is rarely a satisfactory arrangement, particularly for the senior tutor!

Beware of being parochial and confining improvements to your own subject; ensure that lessons learnt are widely disseminated. Also, remember that the quality assessment process itself is a means of disseminating good practice. Assessors will take back to their own institutions and to others they visit what they learn from you.

(f) Action taken in response to evaluation outcomes

Not just about solving problems

There is a wide range of developmental responses to evaluation outcomes. QAE is not simply about detecting and solving problems; it is actually about continuous, professional development of all staff and development of the educational provision. This includes participation in institutional staff development activities; the induction and mentoring of new staff and the continuous professional development of all staff; dissemination of good practice; individual and institutional research into teaching and learning methods; and, indeed, all aspects of the provision.

Judging from quality assessment reports published to date, there is still a long way to go in this area. Apart from the frequent references to failure to 'close the loop' on a whole range of evaluation mechanisms, assessors point to lack of coherent staff development policies, particularly at the subject level. Assessors also note the poor take up of staff development opportunities, especially by experienced staff, and the lack of evaluation of the effectiveness of staff development activities. On the other hand, much good practice has emerged. Some providers have established teaching and learning forums, run workshops and seminars on teaching, and have excellent, sometimes certified, programmes in teaching. Some have codes of practice for teaching and student support. Some providers have responded very promptly and positively to the outcomes of audit and put into place very effective QAE mechanisms.

Assessors will be interested in your arrangements for dissemination of good practice. It is an irony of the quality assessment outcomes that assessors constantly comment on lack of dissemination of good practice and yet this item is not included in the key features for the QAE aspect or its *aide-mémoire*. Dissemination is extremely important, at all levels. There are many dissemination mechanisms to use; such as workshops, publications, newsletters, peer review, and team teaching, and these mechanisms should be an integral part of your quality strategy.

Institutional staff development activities

These are workshops and other activities mounted by a central staff development unit. Most institutions have such a unit, offering a wide range of activities for all categories of staff. The activities are often on topical issues and have the advantage of bringing together staff from across the institution. Recently a large part of academic staff development has been focused on quality assessment, for obvious reasons. Assessors might visit your staff development unit and they will probably want statistics on subject providers' use of the unit. It can be embarrassing that where usage is high it is often related to research rather than teaching!

Central staff development can also fulfil an advisory or facilitative role, assisting in designing and implementing developmental responses to evaluation outcomes. It can put on bespoke courses, consult on an individual basis, or provide facilities for disseminating good practice. Assessors might be interested in the link with central staff development. They particularly favour staff development schemes that cover all categories of staff, including part-time. It helps if every developmental activity has an associated means of evaluating the outcome and its benefit to the student learning experience. The department might have a staff development liaison officer who helps to identify need, disseminate good practice, support development and liaise with central staff development. Does your department provide encouragement and incentives to participate in staff development activities, such as time off, resources or rewards?

Induction and mentoring for new staff

Induction for teaching and learning can range from a two-day 'survival kit' course to a certificated programme of modules covering a range of teaching issues, including projects and action research. A good compromise is an intensive week or two, followed up by regular short courses and seminars, with mentoring and other support. Often the courses come too late, long after the new lecturer has begun teaching, so try to make the initial course as early as possible. Induction courses might be eligible for accreditation by the Staff and Educational Development Association (SEDA), under their Teacher

Accreditation Scheme. The content of the course should be aimed at the practical end initially, with deeper, more theoretical courses when the lecturer has found his or her feet. Encourage the new member of staff to maintain a teaching portfolio.

Assessors have frequently noticed that while induction courses serve full-time academic staff quite well, they do not always reach part-time or technical and administrative staff. In German the induction provision for such staff was deemed inadequate for 20 per cent of providers.

Assessors have observed good practice in the mentoring of new staff. Sometimes such arrangements are linked in a coherent strategy to induction courses and other sorts of training. Mentoring is a difficult and sensitive task, and it should not be assumed that anyone with a few years' experience can do it. Mentors should be carefully selected and undergo a substantial training programme. Team-teaching might work better than a formal mentoring system, because the new member of staff can be effectively mentored by the whole team.

Continuous professional development for all staff

Academics have always been the quintessential example of continuous professional development (CPD). They are used to continually updating themselves on their subject, but not so much on the way they teach it or how they deliver other aspects of the provision. When they had much more time for this, they could afford to do it in an amateurish and uncoordinated manner. Now, however, rapid change and limited resources mean that a minimalist or ad hoc approach is no longer tenable. CPD of academics needs to be organized, supported and resourced. Individual development might need to be linked more closely to institutional strategic plans. Also, the range of activities for professional development will expand, moving away from course-based provision to other modes such as resource-based learning, team-teaching, book groups and portfolios. Quality assessment itself, opening up every aspect of educational provision, is both a motivation and a tool for CPD of all higher education staff. Quality assessment literature, including the reports on the outcomes, provide a wealth of material from which all staff may benefit.

4. Procedural guidelines and record keeping

(g) Procedural documentation

Clear and concise documentation of QAE processes is important. Assessors have noted many examples of poor or non-existent documentation. This is probably a legacy of the previous informal approach to many features of provision in higher education, but it cannot be sustained under the current ethos of accountability. Assessors should be able to consult guidelines, codes of practice, operational instructions and so on, which tell them how any particular QAE mechanism works, who is responsible, how it is resourced and how it is scheduled. These should be as strict as examination regulations, and the day may come when they are indeed subject to the same rigorous regulatory procedures, ratified by institutional committees and ultimately Senate. For the moment assessors will probably accept a simple A4 sheet summarizing the implementation of such things as student questionnaires.

(h) Record keeping

The outcome of any developmental activity should at least be lessons learnt about the provision, if not actual improvements. It is therefore important to keep a record and consolidate the learning into good practice through reports, papers and books. So much of teaching and learning development in higher education is reinventing the wheel because no one recalls that Dr Jones did exactly the same thing five years ago. Keep up with the Joneses by keeping good documentary records.

Much record keeping will be automatic in reports and minutes of relevant committees, external examiners reports, accreditation documentation and so on. In other cases a special effort will be needed, for example in summarizing the outcomes of student questionnaires or peer observation. These can be included in a QAE file for the assessors' convenience.

(i) Allocation of responsibilities

We might have laboured this issue, but assessors have picked up on many occasions where failure to 'close the loop' resulted simply from it being no one's responsibility. Documentation is essential: there should be a documentary record of the lines of responsibility for action, which should be clearly established. When setting up your QAE procedures and infrastructure, establish specific posts with well-defined responsibilities and clear job descriptions. Ensure that due credit is given for the workload involved, and appoint individuals on the basis of their strengths and commitment, not on their availability. Also, give the authority necessary for the responsibility: the post-holder must be empowered to act. Ensure that clear communication links are set up between the various post-holders within the institution. For example, there should clearly be close links with the central quality unit, and with staff development.

(j) Scheduling

Another reason that action often falls by the wayside is that timescales and deadlines are not set. Scheduling of developmental activities is therefore very important. If changes have to be implemented by a certain date, work back from this to determine when the various milestones should be achieved. The key requirement is for prompt and timely response. Often schedules are hamstrung by fixed institutional timetables, such as the dates of various committee meetings; find ways round this, possibly through chairman's action. Sometimes the institutional committee schedule is designed for long-term decision making, such as programme validation, whereas quality issues must be dealt with on a shorter timescale. This might be a case for establishing separate committee structures for quality matters, as indeed some institutions are now doing.

Chapter 10

Preparing for the visit and the visit

This chapter covers:

- the schedule for quality assessment
- an outline of a typical visit
- planning and preparing for the visit
- the preparatory meeting with the reporting assessor
- documentation for the assessment team
- the visit in detail
- evidence gathered by assessors on the visit
- making the most of the visit
- after the visit, including the quality assessment report.

Introduction

Inspection of school provision and classroom observation has long been a feature of the system of assessing school teaching. It is doubtful whether HMI inspectors performing the inspection would feel that they could judge the quality of teaching without actually going into the schools. It is therefore strange that in the first rounds of the HEFCE quality assessment, it was considered possible to decide that teaching quality was 'satisfactory' without so much as setting foot in the institution. Usually institutions were only visited if a claim of 'excellent' was sustained (which lead some institutions to content themselves with a 'satisfactory' claim), or if assessors felt that the quality might be at risk. Although Scottish providers do not have to make such a claim about the quality of their provision, it is interesting to note that they are asked to rate themselves on a 4-point scale. However, this is not for the purpose of determining whether a visit should take place, and the SHEFC-COSHEP Joint Review Group recommend this practice be discontinued (October 1996).

HEFCE has adopted universal visiting since April 1995. The previous system in which a subject provider makes a claim about its provision has been changed to one in which it describes and evaluates the provision, with evidence, and then the assessors come in to assess subjects on that basis. An assessment team analyses the self-assessment document and spends three to four days in your department gathering evidence to make a judgement about the quality of the provision. Assessors delve into every aspect of provision and have virtually unlimited access to stakeholders and documentation.

Schedule for HEFCE quality assessment

The schedule for the overall process of quality assessment is as follows.

Timetable for assessment of subject areas

The HEFCE Circular 20/95 outlines the forward plan for the assessment of subjects up to the year 2001 (HEFCE, 1995a). In Wales the first four-year cycle of assessments will be completed in 1997 and in Scotland the six-year cycle will be completed in 1998. Plans have not been announced beyond these dates.

Subject providers state preferences for timing of visit

The precise timing of the assessment visit is a matter for discussion and agreement between the institution and the Council. HEFCE publishes a circular outlining the preparation for assessment for each round in which you will have a form to complete stating your preference for the academic year to be visited. You can indicate to HEFCE periods in which a visit would be inappropriate, for example the first week of term or at examination time. In fact, you may have to negotiate the best days to visit; for example, you may specifically want to get assessors in to see key elements of the provision that fall outside of the usual Monday afternoon to Thursday afternoon visit. Liaison with HEFCE can be through the quality assessment contact at institutional level or the provider to be assessed.

Notification of intention to visit and request for self-assessment document

HEFCE notifies institutional heads of its intention to visit, a date will be set and you will receive a HEFCE circular informing you of the self-assessment submission date.

Submission of self-assessment document

HEFCE sets the deadline for submissions, based on the term in which the assessment is to be conducted. So, for example, for visits during 1997–98 term 1, a submission was required by 10 April 97, for term 2 by 10 July 97 and for term 3 by 10 November 97. In each case you have up to six months between submitting the self-assessment and the visit. You will be able to provide an update on the self-assessment, so don't worry if things change in this time.

Reporting assessor's preparatory visit to the institution

No later than two months before the assessment visit the reporting assessor visits the institution to work with you in preparation for the visit. The HEFCW equivalent, the quality assessment manager, liaises with institutions over a longer period of time and visits providers on a number of occasions so as to get to know the institution and advise on the self-assessment and visit.

Assessment visit and judgement

The visit itself lasts three to four days, usually Monday to Thursday. Judgement is made by an assessment team, in the form of a graded profile, against which there is no appeal. Feedback is given to the subject provider by the reporting assessor on the last day of the visit. SHEFC is the exception; assessors do not relate the final outcome to the provider at the end of the visit. The judgement appears in a draft report, which is discussed with the senior management of the institution. There is no graded profile; a summative judgement is made on a 4-point scale – unsatisfactory, satisfactory, highly satisfactory and excellent.

First draft report

The reporting assessor and assessment team prepare the quality assessment report, on which you can comment from the point of factual accuracy only. HEFCW stresses the importance of continuing dialogue between the assessment team and the provider beyond the visit. Providers have three opportunities to give feedback on the report (HEFCW, 1996).

Quality assessment report published

Currently, the final quality assessment report should be published within three months of the visit. However, this deadline has proved difficult to meet and a 20-week timetable has now been introduced (HEFCE, 1997b).

Subject overview reports published

HEFCE produces subject overview reports (SORs), which summarize the outcomes of quality assessment for a subject area when the cycle of assessments for each provider of the subject is complete. HEFCW provides a list of outcomes for providers and SHEFC publishes annual reports giving an overview of the findings, feedback on cognate areas and the costings of quality assessment activities.

An outline of the visit

The purpose of the assessment visit

The purpose of the visit is 'to gather, consider and verify the evidence of the quality of education, in the light of the subject provider's aims and objectives in the specific subject, and to achieve a graded profile of the quality of that provision' (HEFCE, 1995b).

The role and activities of the assessment team

At about the time of the preparatory meeting with the reporting assessor, you should be informed of the membership of the assessment team. HEFCE aims to inform providers of assessment team members three months before the visit. Background details of the reporting assessor, and later of the subject specialist assessors, can then be obtained from HEFCE. As soon as you know who they are find out as much as you can about the team and decide whether its expertise covers the diversity of your provision. Like external examiners, assessors have to declare all contacts with your department or institution, including job applications. If you have any objections to individual members or the composition of the team, raise them immediately, in writing and at the most senior level.

HEFCE acknowledges that difficulties are still being experienced in identifying the main characteristics of provision, causing delays in assembling the best team. Some concern has been expressed by institutions about the range of expertise to cover the specialisms taught by the provider. Reporting assessors have rated the appropriateness of the team more highly than have institutions. Providers of some subjects were highly dissatisfied with the cover of specialisms; for example only 39 per cent of respondents from providers of Iberian studies gave positive responses to this question on the evaluation form (Evaluation Questionnaire Part B) issued by the funding council (HEFCE, 1997b). HEFCE is keen to improve the match. Subjects to be assessed between 1998 and 2000 have already been asked to identify the nature of provision to be assessed and nominations for assessors have been invited (HEFCE, 1997a). The Joint Planning Group document (1996) also proposes that heads of institutions could nominate assessment team members against agreed criteria.

The reporting assessor is responsible for managing the assessment team. Contact him or her as early as possible and build up a cooperative working relationship. Under the HEFCW system the quality assessment manager takes charge of all the visits in one institution where possible, which is intended to ensure continuity across subject assessments and to minimize duplication in the coverage of central support services. (An excellent idea!) Also, relationships are built up over an extended period, with the quality assessment manager visiting the institution several times before the assessment visit in order to discuss preparations for the visit and to build up a context for the assessment. SHEFC has a lead assessor, a team of academic assessors and an industrial or lay assessor. Academic assessors perform the same role as HEFCE subject specialist assessors, but a number are recruited from outside of Scotland in order to ensure neutrality and independence. The industrial assessor considers broader vocational issues and social interests of students.

Subject specialist assessors have been chosen to match your provision – curriculum content, the size, whether it is franchized and so on. Usually four to five assessors will visit, depending on the size of your provision and whether you have split sites, for example. Assessors are assigned to different aspects of provision, with responsibility for coordinating the gathering of associated evidence. Naturally this will influence what they do during the visit. Each will convene or attend meetings relevant to their aspect responsibilities; for example, meetings with a quality group or staff development are likely to be conducted by the QAE aspect assessor(s); the tour of computing services, library, laboratories will be conducted by the LR aspect assessor; and tours of central support services such as careers, welfare, health and registry will be conducted by the assessor for the SSG aspect. Depending on the size of the team you may have one assessor or possibly two conducting the meetings.

HEFCW encourages institutions to nominate a member of staff (usually senior academic or administrative member) to be involved in the process. The institution's nominee can observe the visit, making the assessment process more transparent. Such nominees have been used in different ways (UCoSDA and Loughborough University, 1996). Primarily they fulfil the role of an observer and facilitator; they attend meetings and have access to the same documentation as the assessment team, and they provide an institutional perspective. SHEFC recommends that providers have the opportunity to nominate a 'facilitator' to work with the assessment team (SHEFC-COSHEP, 1996).

The assessment team plans the visit based on an analysis of your self-assessment and the documentation sent two weeks in advance of the visit. The *Assessors' Handbook* (HEFCE, 1996a) is clear and precise about the visit. It provides guidance on every part of the visit, including a typical visit schedule and *aide-mémoire* for meetings. It also outlines the activities carried out by an assessment team during the visit, including the following.

- Observation of the various forms of teaching and learning, for example lecture seminar, workshop, tutorial, laboratory, and placement.
- Meetings with academic and administrative/support staff, students, former students and employers where appropriate.
- Scrutiny of institutional and course documents, reviews and reports.
- Scrutiny of student work, for example examination scripts, courseware, projects and dissertations.
- Examination of student learning resources and academic and pastoral support for students.

During the visit, assessors come to a joint decision on the graded profile over the six core aspects of provision.

Planning and preparing for the visit

Your planning and preparation for the visit will depend on when you are going to be assessed. The sooner you start preparing the more time you will have to evaluate your provision and treat the whole quality assessment exercise as a developmental one. Improvements can be planned carefully and monitored, rather than done hurriedly before the visit, or just for the period of the visit!

You can model and develop your provision on the quality assessment framework, incorporating the requirements of quality assessment into your existing quality assurance mechanisms. If you have quality assurance mechanisms that regularly review and develop provision, you will have a good sense of your strengths and weaknesses and have evidence of past improvements. If your quality assurance mechanisms are weak, the exercise of preparing the self-assessment document should reveal this and suggest areas for improvement.

You might have time to address some issues before the self-assessment is submitted, others will have to be addressed between submission and the visit – a minimum of three months. Do not highlight initiatives in the self-assessment if you do not have the time or the resources to follow them through by the time of the visit. Once the visit date has been confirmed by the Quality Assessment Division at HEFCE, the reporting assessor will arrange a preparatory meeting.

Preparatory meeting with reporting assessor

This crucial, formative meeting is the place to ensure that the visit itself is well designed and managed. The meeting will last approximately four hours – make the most of it.

The meeting is an opportunity for the reporting assessor to determine exactly what is being assessed, what documents the assessment team should see in advance, the sample of teaching sessions available for observation, advance meetings and practical arrangements for the visit. It is an opportunity for clarification of the self-assessment, if necessary. Make sure you use the meeting to address any concerns or queries you have and to put your own ideas forward. The meeting should be conducted in a spirit of cooperation and negotiation. The reporting assessor is likely to work to the agenda HEFCE sets for the meeting, but if you do your homework in advance you can influence how the visit is run.

Think carefully about who you would like to attend the meeting; typically five or six staff can attend from the institution. The subject head and subject contact should attend, perhaps two or three senior academic staff from the subject, and, if you have one, the central contact for quality assessment, possibly from a quality assurance unit, staff development or registry. Make sure that staff who attend the meeting are fully conversant with the self-assessment and with key HEFCE literature, such as the *Assessors' Handbook*. The reporting assessor returns a record of the staff attending the preparatory meetings to HEFCE.

Plan how the visit is to be structured, in terms of meetings, tours and the documentation you would like assessors to see. The *Assessors' Handbook* provides a guide to what assessors might ask for in advance and in the base room. You can prepare a list in advance for the reporting assessor to consider at the meeting. This will demonstrate that you are familiar with the quality assessment process and take it seriously. The reporting assessor might seek clarification on your self-assessment and might outline initial impressions. You can provide an update of the document if there is a lengthy period between the submission and the visit.

If any features of your provision are particularly distinctive, make sure the reporting assessor knows about it. If your provision is particularly complex it is helpful to give a short presentation to the assessment team on the first day of the visit to clarify the nature and idiosyncrasies of your provision, and terminology, such as 'programme', 'course' and 'module'. Similarly, if you have a lot of distance or open learning provision, one assessor might work specifically on this. The preparatory meeting is an opportunity for you to give details of any important teaching activity that takes place beyond the nominated visit period, out of hours or on split sites.

Review your departmental timetable to ensure assessors can see a representative sample of teaching activities during the visit. Analysis of the students' timetables for the period of the assessment visit is important. Wholesale reorganization of the teaching timetable before the visit (whatever your intentions) is not advised. Assessors are likely to see this as a disruption for students, and it would probably cause staff confusion too. The best thing to do is to change the days when assessors visit. Do your homework – it should not consume a disproportionate amount of time during the meeting.

There is no HEFCE policy on the layout of a programme timetable, but assessors prefer a timetable designed for their needs on the visit. Would your timetable be intelligible to someone outside your department? One reporting assessor suggested logging the following on an hourly basis from Tuesday 9am to Thursday 1pm: timetable, course, year, subject, lecturers, room and type of class. An assessor who was given timetable information on 34 sheets of paper was not impressed.

At the end of the meeting with the reporting assessor you should feel confident that you know exactly what is going to happen on the visit and that the assessor has the information he or she needs to make appropriate arrangements for the visit. After the meeting the reporting assessor writes confirming the arrangements agreed for the visit. A copy of the letter is sent to the Quality Assessment Division at HEFCE. You will also be asked to complete an evaluation form for HEFCE to provide feedback on the preparatory meeting (Evaluation Questionnaire Part A). Here you can comment on the clarity of information on preparing the self-assessment; the composition of the assessment team; the degree to which a shared understanding was established with the reporting assessor in terms of the range of classes to be assessed; advance documentation, meetings and so on.

Documentation for the assessment team

The assessment team reads documentation in advance of and during the visit. For HEFCE, the documentation is only sent two weeks before the visit. For HEFCW, preliminary information on the programme to be assessed is sent ten weeks before the visit.

The official HEFCE list of documentation required in advance of the visit is:

- a copy of the self-assessment;
- subject information provided for students, for example departmental brochure, course handbooks and leaflets;
- the most recently available subject monitoring, for example internal programme review documentation and/or external examiners' reports;
- timetables for all relevant programmes for the period of the visit;

- university prospectus;
- location map;
- site/building plan;
- staffing list. (Annex C, *Assessors' Handbook*)

You might be asked for other documents in your preparatory meeting. For one meeting we observed, an engineering department also provided a cohort analysis prepared for their professional body (The Institute of Electrical Engineers), industrial training guidelines and a departmental quality plan.

The advance documentation is required so that assessors can start on the particular aspects to which they have been assigned. These documents will be scrutinized carefully (if they are not, assessors are not doing their job properly), so make sure you know them inside out, including the implications for your provision. Having said that, some assessors have not found the self-assessment helpful (HEFCE, 1997b), and it is not uncommon for assessors to ask questions that are clearly answered by the self-assessment. (Or this may be the assessors testing staff to see if they know what is in the self-assessment.) The HEFCW is more rigorous when it comes to the pre-analysis of the self-assessment; assessors are given more time to do it and are issued with a proforma for the purpose. The self-assessment is analysed by assessors and returned to the quality assessment manager four weeks before the visit. The quality assessment manager collates the assessors' analysis of the document and drafts an action plan, suggesting a possible distribution of activities and an agenda for the first meeting of the team. Assessors should not pre-judge the quality of the provision on the basis of the self-assessment; rather they are asked to put forward tentative views and hypotheses about provision, to be tested on the visit.

Consider what impression the assessors will gain about your provision on the basis of the documentation sent to them in advance of the visit. It tells them about your curriculum, your staff, external reviews of your provision, key information given to students and possibly something on your quality assurance procedures. Therefore, they will have some information on the CDCO, SSG and QAE aspects. You could suggest documents that cover other aspects, for example your TLA strategy – the bottom line is to show the department in a good light. Your self-assessment will suggest possible trails for the assessors to follow; think about these in advance and use them as a basis for the documentation you provide.

Documents for the base room

The following documents are listed in Annex C (*Assessors' Handbook*) but do not have to be sent in advance. These documents should be provided in the base room.

Course/programme-related items

- Internal subject monitoring reports for the last three years, including those from professional bodies, students or other sources as appropriate.
- External examiners' reports for the last three years.

Student work

- Samples to reflect the range of courses/programmes, levels and attainment/marks, and to include written work, examination scripts/papers, project/lab reports, dissertations, practical work or other types of work as appropriate (including marking and feedback sheets and assessment criteria).

Statistics/support information

- Staff CVs, details of research and staff development activity, including policy and strategy statements where available.
- Student intake and progression data, covering the last three cohorts.
- A description of student support/welfare services, plus any recent analysis of student use, subject to normal constraints of confidentiality in respect of counselling and similar activities.

Management-related items

- Academic development plans (if available).
- Academic management structure.
- Quality assurance arrangements (including the institution's response to the HEQC audit).
- Summary of the learning resources and accommodation strategy and internal administrative arrangements, library services, general IT and specialist equipment.

There might be many additional items you would like to put in the base room; for example, departmental committee minutes for the last three years, student questionnaires and outcomes, lesson plans of sessions to be observed, copies of handouts given to students, and teaching and learning innovations and their evaluation. You could provide an advance list for the reporting assessor to consider.

If you are asked for student questionnaires or you decide to put them in the base room, make sure you include trails through previous years that show how outcomes of student feedback have been addressed and fed back to students. You could offer feedback to students in classes through a newsletter, a staff–student committee or, better still, by putting something on the questionnaire itself, so students can see that they are benefiting from the feedback of previous students.

Remember that you might have to rush around digging out documentation during the visit if assessors want to follow a particular line of enquiry. So be prepared, have staff available who can put their hands on the documentation; this includes departments like registry, the library and staff development.

Organizing the base room

Organize the base room so it is easy for assessors to find the documents they need. Some have suggested a colour-coded system or organization of material into the six aspects. If you have made specific reference to documentation in the self-assessment under particular aspects, this could be useful. If not, consider the inter-relationship between the aspects and consider how difficult it might be to file! We recommend a simple numbered index of all your documents. You could also have a wall chart in the base room showing study pathways and links between subject programme and course objectives, etc. Make the visit an opportunity to educate the assessors, using all the best means available; you might use visual aids, short talks and resource-based material. Do the sorting and organization for them and communicate as best you can. Under HEFCW the quality assessment manager is guided through the material in the base room; it is a good idea to at least offer to do this.

Provide assessors with functional working conditions; they will need team tables and working tables in the base room and a place for the secretary. Computing facilities do not need to be offered as assessors will bring their own equipment.

The visit in detail

This section focuses in more detail on the HEFCE visit. In principle, the activities of SHEFC and HEFCW visits are similar; the detail is outlined in respective handbooks for assessors. An assessment visit is usually conducted over a period of three to four days, although in particularly complex circumstances it may be extended over a longer period. The schedule is dependent upon the size and location of the provision.

The HEFCE *Assessors' Handbook* (HEFCE, 1996a) provides guidance for assessors on all aspects of the visit including:

- the preparatory meeting
- a typical visit schedule

- notes on practical arrangements for the visit
- an *aide-mémoire* for student meetings
- documentation in advance and in the base room
- agenda for assessment team meetings.

Typically a visit starts on a Monday afternoon with a meeting of the assessment team. This first meeting of the team is for introductions and clarification of roles and responsibilities, and is followed by a welcome from the head of the institution and senior members of staff. This is an opportunity for the aims and objectives of the subject provider to be set into the institutional context.

Assessors have a team meeting at the end of each day and meet regularly throughout the visit in order to share experiences and the evidence they have gathered. Evidence is shared continually and is evaluated in relation to your subject aims and objectives in the self-assessment. The judgement for an aspect is collective and is never made by one person. Typically the reporting assessor meets with the subject contact at the beginning of each day.

Normally the assessment team has an informal and cordial meeting with subject staff on the first day. The team is introduced to teaching staff, identifying those with responsibility for different aspects. The reporting assessor might use this opportunity to dispel some of the quality assessment mythology, such as the over-emphasis on teaching observation, the question of standards and the grading of teaching sessions. Assessors will continue to meet with subject and other staff throughout the second and third day of the visit, with meetings generally lasting one hour at most and concerning the various aspects of provision.

Meetings with students tend to occur at lunch time (when they aren't in lectures), and with employers and past students in the early evening of the second day. Assessors like to see alumni to ask them about their experiences of the complete programme and how useful it has been to them in their careers. They might also invite employers' views of strengths and weaknesses of the course and their involvement in the provision. Although it can be difficult, try to get a representative sample of employers for all programmes.

You need the right sample of students, which may include student representatives, members of the Students' Guild and volunteers. Keep in mind that your sample should be representative in terms of course, level, part-time, full-time, sandwich, mature, foundation, overseas, ethnicity and gender. Student meetings can be split into different programmes, by undergraduate/ postgraduate and by year. Assessors might need separate meetings with students for different purposes, for example to discuss a year abroad or industrial placement. Assessors could start with open questions such as 'What is it like to be a student here?' and then chase any promising lines of enquiry that emerge during the meeting. They are likely to follow up outcomes of the meeting by seeking to investigate such claims as, 'I can't get hold of books or access computers after 8pm'.

In the spirit of continual dialogue, HEFCW assessors will give an oral feedback immediately after meetings have been held. No reference is made to this by HEFCE and it will depend on the reporting assessor, but there is no harm in asking.

Wednesday afternoon is often taken up with tours of facilities, for example of the library, computing services, careers, health, the Students' Guild, sports facilities and registry. Tours of facilities enable assessors to discuss a range of issues including statistics, student usage, purchasing policy, management of resources, links with subject staff and contribution to student study skills. Tours can also include meetings with staff development and registry; depending on what is in the self-assessment and what happens during the visit. Such departments might be informed in advance or be asked for a meeting in response to certain audit trails.

Typically, teaching observation is conducted from 9am Tuesday until 1pm Thursday. Assessors will look at all kinds of teaching and learning activities, for example, lectures, seminars, small-group teaching, workshops and laboratory classes. (See Chapter 5 for more detail.)

Assessors will expect to see a range of student work with respect to level, mode, programme, course, staff and class types. Sampling of student work can be similar to external examination – poor, middle and good work. Assessors are particularly interested in the quality of feedback given to students. HEFCW assessors spend a significant proportion of their time during the visit on reviewing student work. It helps them to form an overall opinion of the standards expected of students and of student achievement. SHEFC states that student work 'is the most visible and immediate evidence of outcomes of the learning process' and stresses that it is *not* an indication of academic standards in the subject (SHEFC, 1997). As part of your quality assurance mechanisms, you could keep a sample of student work every year, for reference purposes.

A key meeting is held between the assessment team and teaching staff at the end of the penultimate day of the visit. This is an opportunity to see how assessors have judged your provision so far, ie their emerging views on quality, including positive features and perceived weaknesses. The judgement should not have been finalized at this point; assessors still gather evidence on the morning of the last day. You can put the record straight if there have been any misinterpretations and you can address factual inaccuracies. However, it is preferable not to be defensive or to provide immediate answers. If the assessors have identified key issues, identify the evidence assessors need to make a complete judgement and give it to them as soon as possible. You might have to scurry around finding the necessary evidence.

HEFCW is much more progressive here: dialogue between the assessment team and the provider is key throughout the visit. Staff are 'able to make a major and formative contribution to the assessment process during the assessment visit' (HEFCW, 1996). The quality assessment manager maintains a continual dialogue with key staff in order to share and test the developing perceptions of the team on the quality of provision.

The team meet on the last day of the visit to review evidence gathered and finalize gradings for every aspect. At the oral feedback meeting on the last day, the reporting assessor announces the grades awarded for each aspect, the strengths and weaknesses for each aspect and rounds off with a set of conclusions roughly as they will appear in the final quality assessment report. The reporting assessor usually gives the positive features first followed by the recommendations. The meeting is for information and factual clarification only – make sure staff are aware of this – as it is important to remember this is not a meeting to argue, dispute or provide further evidence. You can address matters of factual accuracy and the reporting assessor may clarify points you have, and discuss or amplify on behalf of the team. When you receive your quality assessment report there shouldn't be any surprises.

Assessors are reminded in training that they should not, under any circumstances, argue about the validity of any judgements they have made. Additionally, they anticipate issues which may be raised during the feedback meeting and ensure they have evidence to support their judgement. If matters of fact are raised in the meeting (which may have a bearing on the assessors' judgement), these are to be noted without comment at this stage. However, once the grades have been announced at the meeting they will not be changed.

SHEFC does not deliver an outcome to the provider at the end of the visit. This is done at a later date through a draft report which is discussed with the senior management of the institution. HEFCW provides feedback in the closing meeting but dialogue continues between the assessment team and provider while the report is being compiled.

Next we consider the activities of the assessment team in a little more detail, in relation to the nature of the evidence gathered by the team and how it is related to each aspect of provision.

Evidence gathered by the assessment team during the visit

Major sources of evaluative evidence include:

- present and past students
- staff
- external examiners and moderators
- subject peers
- external advisers
- validating and accrediting bodies
- professional bodies
- employers.

The *aides-mémoire* for each aspect are important tools on the visit. Some assessors will work through the questions systematically, others (possibly more experienced) might ad lib a little. HEFCW has taken a clear stance on this and in fact has cut down its *aide-mémoire* in order to minimize its use in a mechanistic fashion.

The self-assessment points to sources of evidence that assessors follow up on the visit and is a guide for the final report. The evidence to support your achievements must be well documented. Experience of quality assessment visits suggest the type of evidence assessors draw on for each aspect throughout the visit, which we summarize below.

Aspect 1: Curriculum design, content and organization (CDCO)

The CDCO aspect sets the scene for assessors and the team receives full details on the curriculum in advance of the visit. This could include the university prospectus, course booklet, leaflets, accreditation documents and syllabus lists. The reporting assessor will want as much detailed information on your curriculum as possible; he or she is interested in how you describe the curriculum to your students. Student work and observation of teaching are also an important source of evidence for the CDCO aspect, providing indicators of the 'level' of material being taught.

Aspect 2: Teaching, learning and assessment (TLA)

Largely this is based on the observation of teaching, scrutiny of student assessment material and review of student work, in the context of a documented TLA strategy, if available.

Aspect 3: Student progression and achievement (SPA)

Student work and statistics, such as student qualifications, progression and employment, form the main evidence for this aspect. Student work is particularly significant under the HEFCW system, which refers more explicitly to standards.

Aspects 4 and 5: Student support and guidance (SSG) and learning resources (LR)

Evidence under both aspects is largely gathered through tours of the department and other university services, including the library, laboratories and computing facilities (LR aspect) and central student support services such as careers, health, central student welfare and counselling (SSG aspect). Assessors will also consider relevant documentation (eg support services documentation for students, library guide) and statistics such as first destination returns and student usage figures.

Aspect 6: Quality Assurance and Enhancement (QAE)

The reporting assessor might ask for any documentation on quality assurance procedures, for example a quality plan at departmental level, at university level or both. Other related documents include the HEQC Audit Report (and response), internal programme reviews, external examiners' reports, outcomes of peer review and staff development literature. Assessors will ask students about their experiences of feedback mechanisms and knowledge of improvements made.

Of course, the six aspects are interrelated, and there will be some overlap in terms of sources of evidence. Poor student achievement could be investigated under each of the six aspects and each might provide an explanation. For example, inappropriate level of content (CDCO aspect); poor assessment and feedback to students (TLA aspect); poor monitoring of student progress (SPA aspect); inadequate student support (SSG aspect); inappropriate allocation of resources (LR aspect); or quality assurance mechanisms which fail to identify and address the problem (QAE aspect). However, the assessment team makes sure that a provider doesn't get penalized twice for the same problem (or rewarded twice for the same strength!)

What makes an effective visit?

Very little guidance is given by HEFCE literature on the visit itself. Building on previous experience, HEFCE has been able to identify certain characteristics that make for effective visits (HEFCE, 1994c). In brief, these are:

- an appropriate number and mixture of SSAs are given to reflect the size, range, nature and scope of the provision;
- thorough preparation for the visit is made in full cooperation between the provider, HEFCE and the reporting assessor;
- information and evidence made available to assessors is accurate, representative and accessible;
- the visit is conducted in a spirit of dialogue and partnership between the provider, the institution and the assessment team;
- the visit starts with a meeting of senior members of the institution to point

out the important characteristics of the provision within an institutional context;

- judgements are collective and based on evidence;
- summary findings of assessors are conveyed clearly at the end of the visit.

We offer a few suggestions on how you can build on this, particularly relating to preparation for the visit, evidence and the conduct of the visit. We have already considered the first two, now we look at how to make the best of the actual visit.

It is helpful for someone, possibly the head of department, to stand back from the visit and get an overview of it. If it appears that the assessment team is veering in the wrong direction, staff can be informed and bring the team back on course. All staff should be familiar with how the visit is to be conducted. You could keep a record of the conduct of the visit, for example whether assessors meet staff before observing sessions; how long they stay (percentage of session); whether feedback is given and whether assessors justify the grade given. A written record will be valuable in the case of an appeal if you feel the visit has not been conducted according to HEFCE protocol.

All staff who contribute to provision need to be available at all times. If key staff are out on secondment, for example, bring them back for the visit. Even if they are not observed teaching they can contribute to the assessment – as a contact person for an aspect, by delivering a presentation to the assessment team, or to help prepare less experienced staff for the visit.

Ensure part-time and visiting staff are present during the visit and are briefed. If it appears that one member of staff is responsible for much of the teaching, such as the senior tutor, assessors will be concerned why this is the case, and they will want to know what contingency plans you have if such a key member of staff fell ill.

All staff should be briefed on the visit and quality assessment in general. The assessment is not something to be left to the head of department or senior tutor. It involves all staff responsible for provision, not just those with specific responsibilities. *Any member of staff involved in the subject provision could be asked questions about any aspect of provision.* Staff need to support each other, so everyone needs to be well informed to avoid contradictions during the visit.

Make sure all appropriate people (internal and external) are available for the period of the visit, including former students, relevant external professional bodies and external examiners. Make sure any 'star performers' are on show – you might be tempted to 'hide' other staff (study leave, conference, early retirement!), but assessors are likely to be wise to attempted cover-ups. Remember to notify and seek the cooperation of departments that provide inward service teaching, institutions involved in franchise arrangements and firms involved in sandwich courses.

Assessors might request additional documentation and possibly additional meetings during the visit, and you should be prepared to be flexible. Such requests should not appear to cause you any difficulty.

Check access to and from the building late at night, and check car parking arrangements (best to avoid clamping of assessors!) Provide a map from the hotel to the campus and think about sign-posting around the department. Will assessors (or anyone else for that matter) be able to find their way around? Are notice boards up to date?

After the visit

Certainly heave a sigh of relief but don't waste an opportunity to capitalize on quality assessment once the dust has settled. No doubt there will have been many improvements to your provision in preparation for quality assessment – this can be a time to consider how to build on them and share your experiences with others. Ensure all those responsible for provision have detailed feedback on the outcome and a commendation for their contribution, including students. No doubt you will want to disseminate a good result, for example in your promotional literature or maybe on the World Wide Web. Reflect on good practice and how this can be shared within the department and the university. Disseminate feedback on the visit to staff in departments due for assessment and to central staff with responsibilities for quality assessment. Reflect on the recommendations and how these can be addressed through the usual quality assurance and enhancement mechanisms.

HEFCE issues the subject provider with an evaluation form (Evaluation Questionnaire Part B) to gain feedback on the visit. As we have mentioned, it is helpful for all staff to monitor the conduct of the visit so you can give a true picture of what happened. This is all the more important if you are unhappy with the conduct of the assessment visit, as you will need evidence to support an appeal. HEFCE wants feedback on the conduct of the visit, including: opportunities to communicate evidence relevant to the evaluation of all aspects; opportunities to respond to issues raised by the team; the role of the self-assessment in the enquiries made during the visit; whether classroom observation protocol was followed; the effectiveness of communication regarding changes to the daily programme and requests for more information and meetings.

The HEFCW also includes monitoring procedures. The Quality Assessment Division at HEFCW monitors the work of quality assessment managers, meeting them on a regular basis and attending assessments at key points during the visit.

Remember that once the grades have been given in the feedback meeting they *cannot* be changed under the HEFCE system: the meeting is factual and it is too late to change the minds of assessors. With respect to the report, the most you can achieve is a change in the emphasis. HEFCW continues dialogue with the provider while the report is being compiled and the provider has three opportunities to provide input. Institutions can submit plans drawn up in the light of assessment including an account of progress to date, which can be appended to the final report. Draft and interim reports are prepared as the basis for further dialogue with the institution.

Quality assessment report

The HEFCE quality assessment report should be published within 12 to 20 weeks of the visit. Immediately after the visit, the reporting assessor assembles the records gathered on the visit and produces a draft report (draft 1), which is then sent to the assessment team for comment. The reporting assessor produces another draft based on comments of the subject specialist assessors (draft 2). This is sent to the administrative officer in the subject team at Bristol. Here the report is reviewed – checked by lawyers and written in HEFCE-speak – and returned with comments.

The reporting assessor incorporates the comments and sends this draft (draft 3) to the provider to check for factual accuracy. You have two weeks to comment on the report and return it to the reporting assessor, who makes the final decision on whether to incorporate your comments. This next draft (draft 4) is returned to the administrative officer at Bristol for a second time. Here the report goes through another two iterations and by the sixth draft the report is sent to the reporting assessor who sends a copy to you. This is the final version that is sent for publication.

Structure of the quality assessment report

The HEFCE quality assessment reports for 1992–95 have five sections: introduction, aims and objectives, student learning experience, student achievement and conclusions. Assessors present their conclusions in two ways, first the positive features, then the recommendations. Positive features are items of provision that have been commended by assessors and recommendations are those items identified for improvement.

The reports for 1995–96 have a different format, which reflects the change in quality assessment methodology. The aims and objectives of the subject provider are quoted verbatim from the self-assessment, followed by a graded profile. The quality of education is outlined under the six aspects of provision and the conclusion remains in the same format – positive features followed by recommendations.

Chapter 11

Conclusion: quality assessment, past and future

This chapter offers discussion of the achievements of quality assessment to date, current concerns about the process and a look into the future. The rapid pace of change of quality assessment makes any sort of critique of the process risky, since it might quickly be overtaken by events. Even the title of this book will be shortly out of date – the name of the process will change, from 'assessment' to 'review'. Although HEFCE has confirmed that assessments in England and Northern Ireland in 1996–98 will be completed under the current methodology, the new Quality Assurance Agency for Higher Education has already been established and moves are afoot to revise procedures (HEFCE, 1997a).

Has quality assessment achieved its objectives?

The purposes of quality assessment detailed in Chapter 1 are to:

(a) secure value for money by assuring the quality of education;
(b) encourage improvements in the quality of education;
(c) provide public information on the quality of education.

Opinions might be mixed on whether or not these are being achieved. We take a personal and relaxed view of each in turn.

(a) Value for money

The outcomes of quality assessment constitute a resounding vote of confidence in the quality of higher education by higher education providers in the

UK (remember that apart from some further education and professional/industrial input, the assessors are themselves higher education providers). In the 1995–96 round, 99 per cent of provision was quality approved; 42 per cent of all grades were 4 and half were 3. The average grade for the SSG aspect was above 3.5 and for the other five aspects of provision, between 3 and 3.5 (HEFCE, 1997b). Only two providers are subject to reassessment due to a grade 1 in the LR aspect.

The apparent level of high quality seems to indicate that HEFCE has achieved its first purpose – securing value for money. Indeed, politicians and taxpayers may wonder how it is that higher education, which is forever complaining about its lack of resources, manages to do such a good job. But how do we know we are *really* getting value for money? Since the unit of resource has declined significantly in recent years, are we to conclude that we were getting less value for money, say, five years ago? If the unit of resource was reduced further, would we get more value for money with little change in quality as measured by quality assessment? The fact is that we have no benchmarks against which to calibrate the value judgements being made. The judgements are by the provider about the provision. Judgements about value for public investment are really matters for the public or the government. However, the public has to rely on the judgements of HEFCE's assessors, who are part of the system.

What about the judgements themselves? Does even the most ivory tower academic really believe that UK higher education is this good? We don't. Some will say 4 does not mean excellent, faultless provision, which may be true but the subtlety will be lost on the average observer. The fact remains that a process of peer assessment which concludes that almost everyone is very good or excellent has got to be suspect. While we do believe that higher education is good value for money, it is not clear to us that quality assessment substantiates the fact.

(b) Encourage improvements

In our mind there is no question that quality assessment has improved educational provision, and will continue to do so, despite claims that the administrative burden it brings has detracted from the teaching. It has both raised the status of teaching and stimulated debate about teaching and learning (HEFCE, 1997b; SHEFC-COSHEP, 1996). Also, HEFCW (1995b) has noted the maturing of institutions in the control and enhancement of quality. Higher education staff are thinking more about the development of educational provision and their own professional development; they also have access to a rich source of material in the outcomes of quality assessment. There are many examples of the increased importance attached to teaching in HEIs due largely to quality audit and assessment: promotion based on teaching; emergence of accredited courses and programmes in higher education teaching;

and sprouting of teaching committees. Developments in teaching and learning and the sharing of good practice across the sector have also been stimulated by the Fund for the Development of Teaching and Learning (FDTL). In the first phase of this initiative 44 projects were funded and 35 projects have proceeded to the second stage of the second phase of bids (£8 million in total for 1996–98).

There is a danger, however, that if the outcomes of quality assessment continue to be so impressively favourable, it could undermine the second purpose of the process; the results could lead to complacency in the sector, rather than encourage improvement. Once providers have learnt how to play the game and everyone gets good, what is the incentive to improve? The process itself could breed conformity and a compliance culture, encouraging providers to 'crib for the exam'.

(c) Provide public information

Perhaps the greatest bonus of the quality assessment process lies in the enormous published output of education activity in the higher education sector – the quality assessment reports. These represent a tremendous resource, which amply supports the second and fulfils the third purposes of HEFCE quality assessment. It provides a wealth of material to help institutions in their own research and educational development and for sector-wide research. This book contains many examples of how all stakeholders can benefit from the goldmine. In designing the staff development plan for our own institution we have used the quality assessment outcomes to identify priority areas and good practice. We are confident that the third objective has been achieved. The question is then…

Is it worth the expense?

Some might argue that a lot of money has been wasted on proving that virtually all higher education provision is quality approved. The direct cost of quality assessment to HEFCE in the early rounds was £3 million in 1993–94 and £3.7 million in 1994–95, most of which was attributed to the training and support of assessors and Quality Assessment Division staff costs. To put these figures in perspective, the direct cost in 1994–95 amounted to less than 0.1 per cent of the total public funding (HEFCE grant and tuition fees) for teaching (HEFCE, 1995e). This is a small sum to pay for what is intended to account for the quality of publicly funded provision, as well as provide instruments for the dissemination of good practice and informing the public. It is not uncommon for institutions to spend, proportionately, ten times this amount on their normal staff development. Why then the howls of protest from some quarters about the costs?

Of course, HEFCE costs do not include those incurred by the institutions in responding to quality assessment, which is the cost that hurts at the provider and institutional level. Stories of senior staff spending months in preparation are common: 'senior staff were effectively immobilized for a long stretch of time' (UCML, 1996). However, if the response to quality assessment is coordinated properly at the institutional level, only the initial set-up costs need be significant. Once the systems, documentation and personnel are in place, the costs during subsequent rounds should be minimal.

Another complaint is that the energy and expense employed in responding to quality assessment would have been better spent on development of teaching – but would provision have been developed to the same extent without an external stimulus?

In our opinion the increase in the profile of teaching and the wealth of information disseminated in the quality assessment reports are well worth the cost. This is not to say that there isn't room for improvement; hopefully cost savings will be made by combining the assessment and audit processes under the new QAAHE. However, the Joint Planning Group Report (1996) is not entirely convincing in this respect. It appears that audit and assessment have been bolted together and given new names ('institution-wide review' and 'subject/programme review', respectively) without fully integrating the two. However, the work of the QAAHE is only just starting and it has a good foundation on which to build: the outcomes of quality assessment, feedback from evaluation mechanisms and the response of the Welsh and Scottish funding councils to the Joint Planning Group proposals.

The commitment of the funding councils to continually develop the methodology is illustrated by the extensive consultation exercises undertaken so far (CHES, 1994; HEFCW, 1994b, 1995b; SHEFC-COSHEP, 1996). The methodology has evolved with impressive rapidity, for example the introduction of the six core aspects and the replacement of a summative judgement with a graded profile. Also, evaluation of the process is becoming more formalized. As a result HEFCE has recognized the need for improvement in the following areas: the speed of report production; institutional perceptions of the opportunities to comment on issues raised by the team during the visit; delays in confirming team membership with institutions; matching team composition to the nature and size of the provision (HEFCE, 1997b). To its credit, HEFCE has shown itself willing and able to continually adapt and improve its procedures, for example in the introduction of the equal opportunities policy (HEFCE, 1997b) and the early request for assessors and information from providers to be assessed in 1998–2000 (HEFCE, 1997a).

Overall, therefore, we believe that the quality review (née audit plus assessment) process is worth the expense, and we are impressed by the rapidity of its development and the clear commitment to improvement. However, we are still worried about some aspects of the exercise.

What aspects of quality assessment cause concern?

It is understandable that any attempt to assess the quality of educational provision in higher education will attract criticism. In the early days of assessment everyone had their own horror story to tell – the assessor falling asleep in a lecture, the incompetent or rude assessor, the assessor trying to poach staff – anecdotes abound (UCML, 1996).

There are many sources of criticism of the early quality assessment methodology, in particular Alderman's review of the process in England (Alderman, 1996); a formal complaint made to HEFCE by a former subject assessor on behalf of the English Association (Campbell, 1995); and, more recently, the University Council for Modern Languages prepared a report entitled *Assessing the Assessors* (UCML, 1996). The concerns raised include: the cost of the exercise; the inadequacy of the selection and training of assessors; inappropriate behaviour of some assessors; failure of assessment teams to recognize mission statements such as 'access' and 'service to the community'; ineffectiveness of administrative procedures; and general inconsistencies that are considered to invalidate the process.

The UCML report indicates that many providers tend not to complain; for example, despite the fact that 59 per cent of English providers surveyed were dissatisfied with its membership, only half sought changes to the assessment team. Is this simply because providers are not aware of their right to appeal or does a favourable result render such a response unnecessary or undesirable? Not surprisingly, a consultation exercise with providers in Scotland showed that satisfaction with the visit was much higher among departments which received an 'excellent' (SHEFC-COSHEP, 1996).

Some of these criticisms are of the old, less effective methodology, which have now been addressed. However, some fundamental concerns remain, which we believe need to be dealt with if the new quality review system is to maintain credibility.

Lifetime of the graded profile

One of the major weaknesses of the current system is the long cycle time. At present, once a graded profile is awarded, it is fixed for eight years, which is a positive disincentive to improvement. No one will bother to put effort into developmental activities arising from the outcomes of quality assessment when the next opportunity for improving the profile is eight years away. Conversely, a department that gets a perfect graded profile might well lose staff within a few years and the quality of the provision could deteriorate, but the misleading profile remains intact.

It is unlikely that the main cycle time will be reduced, but it should be possible to have an updating procedure whereby evidence of the response to recommendations identified can earn remission on the graded profile.

Crude numerical measures

HEFCE emphasizes that the aggregation of quality assessment aspect scores is not appropriate, but inevitably providers and stakeholders will view scores in aggregate. League tables will emerge and 22 out of 24 will be regarded as better than 19 out of 24. The *Times Higher Education Supplement* has already published league tables showing mean TQA scores (*THES*, 23 May 1997). (Welsh providers have also been included in the tables, despite their use of colours.) This is one of the worst aspects of the quality assessment procedure in higher education – league tables are hardly conducive to effective self-evaluation and development. We wonder whether anyone with experience of the HEFCE system would believe that it is sufficiently rigorous to provide accurate resolution on what is effectively a 24-point scale. HEFCE indicates for example that the new profiling method distinguishes less strongly between former UFC and former PCFC institutions (HEFCE, 1997b). We argue that it distinguishes less strongly between all providers. Is a provider with an aggregate 19 points clearly distinguishable from one with 21 points? Since there is no attempt to monitor the comparability of standards between different teams in the same subject area (Alderman, 1996), and in view of the low confidence in the reliability of judgements that has been expressed in some quarters (SHEFC-COSHEP, 1996), we have to say no. It is for the worse, of course, that providers are stuck with these unreliable scores for so long.

The selection and training of assessors

This issue is vital to the credibility of the system. We recognize the improvements made to the training of assessors, but we feel there is still a long way to go. As one provider puts it, 'How can three days' training match the training that former HMI inspectors had before they observed teaching?' (UCML, 1996). Is the HEFCE requirement to have a knowledge of higher education and an understanding of current teaching and learning methods sufficient? There are many accredited teaching qualifications in higher education now and it is not inconceivable that the bulk of a department could be more highly qualified than the assessors assessing them. The schedule of assessments is known well in advance and there is no excuse for not providing very substantial training for the assessors.

On the matter of selection this has caused us some concern. In our work on quality assessment on too many occasions we have been surprised by selections and rejections made. One lecturer chosen as an assessor had been recently removed from a course as a result of student protest, and had been castigated by the head of department at an exam board for failing to provide examination results because he had been away on a research conference. Conversely, superior dedicated and experienced teachers have been rejected. Of course, anecdotal evidence is neither valid nor reliable, but such experiences are still unsettling.

The assumption appears to be that the selected assessors are as experienced and expert in teaching as the average academic, and that the purpose of the training is to prepare them for making the assessment using this experience and expertise. This is the nature of peer review, and one might argue that it works well in research, so why not in teaching? In research, peers are usually comparably expert in the subject, but in teaching very few academics are experts at all – they have never been trained and until now nobody has cared much about their teaching capabilities.

Assessors need to be credible – indeed, impressively so – to carry any conviction in the quality assessment exercise. The really serious consequence of any lack of credibility of assessors is not that assessors will err on the hard side, but that they will be easily hoodwinked by providers once they have the measure of the situation. The result will be that the exercise, far from enhancing quality, will allow institutions to continue providing indifferent education under a worthless seal of approval. Perhaps this is already happening, in view of the flatteringly high grades being awarded.

HEFCE has made some progress in the area of selection and training. For example, the training programme has been revised, there is a greater degree of evaluation of the methodology (HEFCE, 1997b) and nominations for assessors are being invited much earlier (HEFCE, 1997a). It is interesting to note that training in Scotland is undertaken by the Council but in England and Northern Ireland it is subcontracted.

In Scotland the current process is considered to have a number of shortcomings and there is clearly some resentment of the process with a few cases of damaged relations with the funding council. In a consultation exercise (with heads of department, academic staff and students, etc) only 22 per cent of respondents were confident that a different team of assessors assessing the same department would come to the same judgement about teaching quality (SHEFC-COSHEP, 1996). The report makes a number of recommendations to improve the credibility of the process. Examples include that institutions should have a limited right of veto on team members; appointment of a professional assessor who might advise teams and a facilitator to advise teams on factual matters, etc; removal of single rating which militates against the developmental aspects of the process; and reduction of the number of aspects to those most directly relevant to the student learning experience.

Terminology

Anxious not to appear prescriptive, HEFCE has avoided rigorous definitions of the terminology used in quality assessment literature. We would be hard pressed to find an example of universally agreed teaching and learning terminology in higher education, so why should HEFCE's be accepted as the last word? That said, the terminology that HEFCE does define is not always clear and consistent, for example in relation to learning outcomes and TLA strategies. This is particularly clear on reading the quality assessment reports. We doubt that many assessors or providers can interpret HEFCE terminology unambiguously. In the interests of good communication (and indeed, good education) HEFCE should publish a full glossary of the terms and definitions it uses, with examples if necessary. Far from feeling imposed on, we suspect that most providers would be grateful for the clarification.

What can we expect in the foreseeable future?

Advocate for the sector?

The recent survey of staff in institutions reported in HEFCE Council Briefing No. 7, 1997, indicated a clear desire among academics to see the Council acting more like a partner or advocate for the higher education sector. Enhancing dialogue with institutions at the educational level and building on the quality assessment outcomes would seem to be a good way of doing this. The FDTL-funded projects will go some way towards facilitating this process, but an established base and presence linked to HEFCE would be a more permanent repository of research and good practice. The funding councils could be more proactive and interventionist in developing and disseminating outcomes of quality assessment, perhaps by establishing an institute dedicated to the purpose. This would enable the QAAHE to collate and benefit from all the good practice in England, Northern Ireland, Wales, Scotland and in further education, and to research how best to ensure the developmental effectiveness of the quality review process.

Funding and quality

The outcomes of the early methodology show clear differences between former PCFC and former UFC institutions; for example of the 26 per cent of providers judged to be excellent, over three-quarters were former UFC, with less than a quarter former PCFC. Of those judged excellent 71 per cent also had an RAE rating of 5 (HEFCE, 1995e). The correlation between teaching excellence and good research ratings was considered to be an embarrassment to the government (Alderman, 1996).

Under the post-April 1995 system the outcomes of the profiling method make less distinction between the two former UFC and PCFC sectors, with the exception of the learning resources aspect. For former PCFC institutions, about a quarter achieved a grade 2 or less for this aspect. Thus, there is still a hint that there might be a link between the funding of provision and the quality that can be achieved, which disadvantages the former PCFC providers. Perhaps this is not unrelated to recent proposals that the LR aspect should be dropped (*THES*, 4 April 1997).

The funding method for teaching is under review (HEFCE, 1995f), and it can only be a matter of time before funding is linked to quality assessment (or review) outcomes. The only current example of linking the outcomes of quality assessment to funding is in the Scottish system. It is SHEFC policy to reward institutions assessed as 'excellent' in educational provision for a cognate area, with 5 per cent additional funded numbers in the appropriate subject area. However, it has been suggested that a proportion of this should be transferred to a fund for the 'development of teaching and learning quality' to which institutions could submit proposals (SHEFC-COSHEP, 1996).

The new Quality Assurance Agency for Higher Education

The QAAHE was set up in April 1997, designed to bring together quality assessment and audit. It is too early to say much about how it will operate or the impact it will have on quality in higher education but the Joint Planning Group report (JPG, 1996) has some pointers to this.

The immediate task of the agency will be to ensure that the momentum of current assessment and audit programmes is maintained, and to pilot, develop and consult on developments in the process. The new agency will take over all the functions of the HEQC and the main assessment functions of those funding councils choosing to contract with the agency for the discharge of those functions.

The intention is for the review process to include institutional provision 'wherever and however delivered, and however funded' (JPG, 1996). The process will assess the extent to which the institution is discharging its responsibilities for teaching and learning at subject/programme level; indicate areas of strength and weakness; evaluate the *validity and reliability* of an institution's internal review procedures; and provide reassurance that each institution has in place effective arrangements for assuring the *academic standards* in the institution. Yes, *standards*, which we have studiously avoided discussing in this book, will become a major issue – the source of another book at least.

Some of the key elements of the Joint Planning Group's proposals for an integrated process of quality assurance are as follows.

- An *institutional quality assurance programme* agreed with the agency, setting out the educational provision to be reviewed over the *eight-year cycle* and *reflecting the institution's own priorities, educational provision and academic structures.*
- Flexibility for each institution to agree with the agency the number, scope and timing of reviews to enable an *institutional perspective* to be brought to bear on the process from the outset, and ensure that the agency and the institution can *harmonize internal and external review arrangements.*
- The opportunity for each institution to *combine subject/programme reviews* within the agreed institutional quality assurance programme, thereby reducing the number of 'engagements' with the agency.
- The timing of subject/programme area reviews to accommodate the accreditation arrangements of the PSBs, where relevant, thus allowing scope for greater collaboration with such bodies.
- Confirmation of the extent to which an institution as a whole is discharging its educational responsibilities and has procedures securely in place that will enable it to continue to do so.

SHEFC and HEFCW responses to the Joint Planning Group report

It is intended for the QAAHE to have a UK-wide remit and the Joint Planning Group report stressed the importance of taking full account of national requirements and educational arrangements in different parts of the UK. We finish, therefore, with the views of HEFCW and SHEFC on the Joint Planning Group proposals (HEFCW, 1995b; SHEFC-COSHEP, 1996).

Higher Education Funding Council for Wales (HEFCW)

HEFCW has signed up to the new agency but wishes to retain some of the distinctive features of the Welsh system. For example, HEFCW has made considerable progress in establishing partnerships that are non-inspectorial and conducted in the spirit of dialogue between peers. HEFCW suggests more involvement of institutions in the process, in order to avoid unnecessary duplication of separate external and internal QAE processes. It also stresses the importance of a robust self-evaluation for real quality assurance which remains valid over time. HEFCW suggests that external assessment could be reduced for those institutions which are able to provide evidence of maturity and commitment to QAE. HEFCW considers the proposed review cycles to be too long and suggests that the outcomes of the assessment exercise should have a sell-by date. The new agency needs to ensure the complementarity of the audit and assessment processes and must address the issue of standards (HEFCW, 1995b).

Scottish Higher Education Funding Council (SHEFC)

On the relationship between audit and assessment, the joint review group (SHEFC-COSHEP, 1996) acknowledges the development of review mechanisms within institutions, and makes the following recommendations: audit should not be routinely applied to aspects of provision fully covered by assessment; there is a case for audit where proven weaknesses are identified by assessment; there is a role for institution-wide review for areas such as modularization, the Credit Accumulation and Transfer Scheme (CATS), work-based learning and collaboration with other institutions at home and abroad. At the time of writing SHEFC has not yet agreed whether to join the new agency.

Issues/evidence grids

This appendix gives examples of the use of issues/evidence grids for each aspect. We have selected a few sources of each type from the categories specified in Chapter 2. You might think of many more in your own particular context, and we have left a few blank columns for you to complete as an exercise. The issues broadly follow those stated in Chapters 4–9, but again you can add or adapt as appropriate. The ticks denoting sources of evidence for each issue are, of course, relevant to a specific provision and your grids might look very different – for example, you might not have an accreditation column, or your external examiner could comment on a wider range of issues.

**Aspect 1
Curriculum design, content and organization**

1. Structure and content of curricula

2. Intended outcomes of curricula

3. Currency and innovative features

Aspect	Accreditation	External examiners' reports	HEQC audit	Employers		Internal programme review	Library services	Careers service	Assessment results	Attrition statistics	Students' work	Student question-naires	Peer observation
(a) Special characteristics of the provision	✓	✓				✓	✓	✓			✓	✓	
(b) Breadth, depth and coherence	✓	✓				✓					✓	✓	
(c) Match of curriculum to student profile, progression and achievement	✓	✓				✓		✓	✓	✓	✓	✓	
(d) Flexibility and student choice	✓	✓		✓		✓					✓	✓	
(e) Specialisms of academic staff	✓					✓						✓	
(f) Clearly defined and communicated intended outcomes of teaching and learning	✓	✓	✓			✓						✓	
(g) Learning opportunities – subject-specific and generic/transferable skills	✓			✓		✓	✓				✓	✓	
– vocational competencies and employment	✓			✓		✓		✓			✓	✓	
– progression to further study	✓					✓		✓			✓	✓	
– personal development	✓			✓				✓					
(h) In the subject and in teaching and learning	✓	✓	✓	✓									
(i) Informed by professional activities of staff	✓			✓									

Aspect 2 Teaching, learning and assessment	Accreditation	External examiners' reports	HEQC audit	Employers	Internal programme review	Library services	Careers service	Assessment results	Attrition statistics	Students' work	Student question-naires	Peer observation
1. Teaching, learning and assessment strategy												
(a) Match of TLA activities to learning objectives	✓				✓							
(b) Match of TLA activities to curriculum	✓				✓							
(c) Implications for student workload	✓				✓			✓	✓		✓	
(d) Implications for student support and guidance	✓				✓		✓					
(e) Implications for learning resources	✓				✓	✓					✓	
(f) Match of provision to student profile	✓				✓						✓	
(g) Strategy documented and understood by staff and students?	✓		✓		✓						✓	
2. Observation of teaching and learning activities												
(h) Description of the teaching and learning activities observed (assessors only)												
(i) Strengths and weaknesses of TLA activities											✓	✓
3. Student assessment												
(j) Assessment criteria and effectiveness of assessment methods	✓	✓			✓			✓		✓	✓	
(k) Assessment as an aid to student learning	✓	✓			✓			✓		✓	✓	
(l) Feedback on students' work	✓	✓			✓			✓		✓	✓	

Aspect 3 Student progression and achievement	Accreditation	External examiners' reports	HEQC audit	Employers		Internal programme review	Library services	Careers service		Assessment results	Attrition statistics		Students' work	Student question-naires		Peer observation
1. Student profile																
(a) Description of student profile	✓					✓										
(b) Match of student profile to subject aims	✓		✓			✓										
(c) Policy and criteria for student access	✓		✓			✓								✓		
2. Progression and completion rates																
(d) Data and trends in progression	✓	✓				✓				✓	✓		✓			
(e) Procedures for addressing poor progression	✓	✓				✓					✓					
(f) Transfer rates in and out of the subject	✓					✓				✓	✓					
(g) Qualifications awarded	✓	✓	✓			✓										
3. Student achievement																
(h) Internal evidence of students' achievements	✓		✓			✓							✓			
(i) External evidence of students' achievements	✓		✓			✓	✓									

Aspect 4 Student support and guidance	Accreditation	External examiners' reports	HEQC audit	Employers	Internal programme review	Library services	Careers service	Assessment results	Attrition statistics	Students' work	Student question-naires	Peer observation
(a) Student support and guidance strategy	✓		✓		✓	✓	✓				✓	
(b) Documentation for students	✓		✓		✓	✓					✓	
(c) Identifying and meeting individual student's needs	✓		✓		✓						✓	
(d) Departmental and institutional provision	✓		✓		✓	✓	✓				✓	
(e) Staff-student relations	✓				✓						✓	
(f) Arrangements for student admission and induction	✓		✓		✓	✓					✓	
(g) Arrangements for academic guidance and tutoring	✓				✓							
(h) Arrangements for pastoral and welfare support	✓				✓						✓	
(i) Arrangements for career guidance	✓				✓		✓				✓	

Aspect 5 Learning resources	Accreditation	External examiners' reports	HEQC audit	Employers	Internal programme review	Library services	Careers service	Assessment results	Attrition statistics	Students' work	Student question-naires	Peer observation
1. Learning resources strategy												
(a) Learning resources strategy	✓		✓		✓	✓					✓	
(b) Liaison with subject and central support	✓				✓	✓					✓	
2. Library resources												
(c) Availability and accessibility	✓		✓		✓	✓					✓	
(d) Induction and ongoing user support	✓				✓	✓					✓	
(e) Books, periodicals, etc	✓				✓	✓					✓	
3. Equipment and IT												
(f) Availability and accessibility	✓		✓		✓						✓	
(g) General and specialist equipment	✓				✓						✓	
(h) Learning materials, for example TLTP	✓				✓	✓					✓	
(i) Induction and ongoing user support	✓				✓						✓	
4. Teaching and social accommodation												
(j) Suitability of accommodation	✓				✓						✓	
5. Technical and administrative support												
(k) Technical and administrative support	✓				✓						✓	

Aspect 6 Quality assurance and enhancement	Accreditation	External examiners' reports	HEQC audit	Employers	Internal programme review	Library services	Careers service	Assessment results	Attrition statistics	Students' work	Student question-naires	Peer observation
1. Quality assurance and enhancement strategy												
(a) Documentation and ownership of strategy	✓		✓	✓	✓						✓	✓
(b) Provision assured by the strategy	✓		✓	✓	✓						✓	✓
2. Evaluating the provision												
(c) What evaluation methods are used?	✓		✓	✓	✓						✓	✓
(d) Are the evaluation methods valid and reliable?	✓		✓	✓	✓						✓	✓
3. Developing the provision												
(e) Infrastructure for taking action	✓		✓	✓	✓						✓	✓
(f) Forms of action taken	✓		✓	✓	✓						✓	✓
4. Procedural guidelines and record keeping												
(g) Are procedural guidelines documented?	✓		✓	✓	✓						✓	✓
(h) Maintenance of records	✓		✓	✓	✓						✓	✓
(i) Lines of responsibility	✓		✓	✓	✓						✓	✓
(j) Scheduling of QAE mechanisms	✓		✓	✓	✓						✓	✓

SCONUL/UCISA *aide-mémoire* for assessors

Evaluating library and computing services

(a) Integration and liaison

(i)   How do the library and computing services become aware of course development and review?

(ii) Do these arrangements work well, meeting the real needs in a timely fashion?

(iii) How do the library, computing, and teaching staff communicate with each other, and how well does this work?

(iv) How do the library and computing staff communicate with students, and how well does this work?

(v)   In what ways are students and staff encouraged and enabled to make effective use of the range of library and computing services available?

(b) Provision for the courses being assessed

The following issues of quantity and quality of provision could be explored together with discussions about how any perceived difficulties are being addressed, with the aims and objectives in the self-assessment document as the principal point of reference.

(b1) Relevance of learning materials

(i) Are the available library and computing resources appropriate (quality) and sufficient (quantity) to support the taught courses, in particular in respect of books and periodicals, software, datasets, and equipment?

(ii)   How are these learning resources, and their means of delivery, selected and updated?

(b2) Availability and accessibility

(i)   How well matched are the availability and locations of the services to the needs of the students?

(ii)   How accessible are the library and IT facilities for all groups of students (eg part-time, disabled, distance learning)?

(iii)   How adequate (quantity) and suitable (quality) is the library study accommodation for student needs?

(iv)   How adequate (quantity) and suitable (quality) are the workstation and other computing and data networking facilities for student needs?

(b3) User support

(i)   What skills training is offered to students and staff?

(ii)   What arrangements are in place for promoting services and responding to enquiries? How effective are they?

(iii)   What steps are taken to enhance and update skills of library and computing staff in order to ensure the quality of support services?

(c) Evaluation and feedback

(i)   How are the relevance and effectiveness of library and computing services to the courses evaluated?

(ii)   How is this fed back into service improvement?

This *aide-mémoire* was published by the Standing Conference of National and University Libraries (SCONUL, 102 Euston Street, London NW1 2HA) in October 1996, and was produced on behalf of SCONUL, UCISA (Universities and Colleges Information Systems Association) and HCLRG (Higher Education Colleges Learning Resources Group). It was written by Jean Sykes, with the help of Nik Pollard, Scott Robertson and Kenneth Heard. David Bradbury, Associate Director of the Higher Education Funding Council for England, wrote of the *aide-mémoire* in a letter to Jean Sykes dated 8 October 1996:

'A copy has now been sent to all our Reporting Assessors and will be available to the subject assessors responsible for the learning resources aspect. It will be used to reinforce and endorse what is said in the assessor handbook concerning learning resources. A copy has also been sent to our UCoSDA trainers who will alert assessors to the purposes of the *aide-mémoire*.

'I very much appreciate the assistance that you and SCONUL have given to us and hope that when it comes to planning for the new method under the single quality agency you will be able to offer us further help.'

Appendix III

Directory of addresses and resources

Centre for Higher Education Practice (CHEP)
The Open University, Walton Hall, Milton Keynes, MK7 6AA.
Tel: 01908 858437; e-mail: chep@open.ac.uk

Centre for Higher Education Studies
Institute of Education, 55–59 Gordon Square, London, WC1H 0NT.
Tel: 0171 612 6363; www site: http://www.ioe.ac.uk
Offers a range of workshops on teaching and learning in higher education. CHES conducted an external evaluation of the quality assessment methodology in 1994.

Committee of Vice-Chancellors and Principles (CVCP)
Woburn House, 20 Tavistock Square, London, WC1H 9HQ
Tel: 0171 419 4111; www site: http://www.cvcp.ac.uk/
The CVCP consists of the executive heads of universities in the UK. It represents universities in dealing with government, funding councils and other national institutions, providing information and services. It aims to promote understanding of universities' aims, needs and achievements and to assist in developing and sharing good practice. It has six specialist agencies to which specific functions have been assigned: UCoSDA, UCEA (Universities and Colleges Employers Association), UCAS, HESA, CSU (Higher Education Careers Services Unit), and HEQC.

Department for Education and Employment (DfEE)
Sanctuary Buildings, Great Smith Street, London, SW1P 3BT
Tel: 0171 925 5000; www site: http://www.open.gov.uk/

Department of Education for Northern Ireland (DENI)
Rathgael House, Balloo Road, Bangor, County Down, BT19 7PR
Tel: 01247 279 279; www site: http://www.deni.gov.uk

Further Education Development Agency (FEDA)
Head Office, 1st Floor, Dunbarton House, 68 Oxford Street, London, W1N 0DA
Tel: 0171 436 0020; www site: http://www.feda.ac.uk/
Publishes a wide variety of material (see the Information Services home page for details) and provides a programme of courses and conferences for college staff and manages a range of research and development projects, working closely with the further education sector and other key education and training organizations. The material is valuable for the subject of this book in that it contains a wealth of good practice from which higher education can learn.

Higher Education Funding Council for England (HEFCE)
Northavon House, Coldharbour Lane, Bristol, BS16 1QD
Tel: 0117 931 7317; www site: http://www. hefce.ac.uk/
The quality assessment function of HEFCE has been taken over by QAAHE, but the HEFCE material is likely to be valuable for some time to come. Publications include circulars setting out quality assessment guidelines, assessors' handbooks, quality assessment reports and overview reports and other material (see Chapter 2).

Higher Education Funding Council for Wales (HEFCW)
Lambourne House, Cardiff Business Park, Llanishen, Cardiff, CF4 5GL
Tel: 01222 761 861; www site: http://www.niss.ac.uk/education/hefcw/
HEFCW produce various circulars, guidelines and reports for assessment. For the current methodology see *Higher Education Funding Council for Wales Quality Assessment Programme 1996/97: Guidelines for Assessment*.

Higher Education Quality Council (HEQC)
344–354 Gray's Inn Road, London, WC1X 8BP
Tel: 0171 837 2223; www site: http://www.niss.ac.uk/education/heqc/
The HEQC was set up in 1992 to maintain quality and standards. Now incorporated into the QAAHE, the future of this resource is uncertain. However, HEQC's publications list, list of audit reports and an order form can be accessed on its website.

Higher Education Statistics Agency (HESA)
18 Royal Crescent, Cheltenham, Gloucestershire, GL50 3DA
Tel: 01242 255577; www site: http://www.hesa.ac.uk/
Provides a statistical service to HEIs in the UK, to higher education funding councils and to government education departments. Data includes information on students, staff and finance. The units of assessment are currently based on HESA codes.

National Information Services and Systems (NISS)
CHEST and NISS Centre, University of Bath, Claverton Down, Bath, BA2 7AY
Tel: 01225 826 145; www site: http://www.niss.ac.uk/
NISS is an information service, providing a focal point for education and research communities in the UK. The NISS information gateway links users to a wide range of services on the Internet and other networks.

National Union of Students (NUS)
461 Holloway Road, London, N7 6LJ
Tel: 0171 272 8900; www site: http://www.nus.org.uk/
The NUS represents the interests of students in further and higher education throughout the UK. It provides training for individual students and student unions, including literature on quality issues and training material for student representatives.

Oxford Centre for Staff and Learning Development (OCSD)
Oxford Brookes University, Gipsy Lane, Headington, Oxford, OX3 0BP
Tel: 01865 484 617; www site: http://www.brookes.ac.uk/
Well known for its developmental activities in higher education, the OCSD offers a wide programme of courses and workshops on a regular basis and publishes books on all aspects of teaching and learning.

Quality Support Centre (QSC)
The Open University, 344–354 Gray's Inn Road, London, WC1X 8BP
Tel: 0171 447 2506; www site: http://www.open.ac.uk/ou/admin/qsc.html
The QSC is a research team at the Open University. It was commissioned by HEFCE to report on the outcomes of quality assessment between 1992 and 1995, focusing on recommendations for improvement.

Staff and Educational Development Association (SEDA)
Gala House, 3 Raglan Road, Edgbaston, Birmingham, B5 7RA
Tel: 0121 440 5021; www site: http://www.seda.demon.co.uk/
Set up in 1993 when the Standing Conference on Educational Development joined with the

SRHE's Staff Development Group to develop a professional standard in higher education teaching. Conducts workshops and conferences, relating to all aspects of development in higher education and has a teacher Accreditation Scheme for programmes of training lecturers, recognizing 60 programmes to date. SEDA publishes books and reports, *The New Academic* magazine and a journal, *Innovations in Education and Training International* (IETI).

The School of Independent Studies
Lancaster University, Lancaster, LA1 4YN
Tel: 01524 593 888; www site: http://www.lancs.ac.uk/users/indstud/
The School of Independent Studies at Lancaster houses the IHE (Innovations in Higher Education) which publishes a paperback series describing students' experiences of university education. The school also has a Professional Development Unit which provides short courses on a range of topics including quality assessment and the QAAHE.

Scottish Higher Education Funding Council (SHEFC)
Donaldson House, 97 Haymarket Terrace, Edinburgh, EH12 5HD
Tel: 0131 313 6500; www site: http://www.shefc.ac.uk/
SHEFC produces various circulars, guidelines for assessment and reports. For the current methodology see *Scottish Higher Education Funding Council Quality Assessment 1997–98*.

Society for Research into Higher Education (SRHE)
3 Devonshire Street, London, W1N 2BA
Tel: 0171 637 2766; e-mail: srhe@clus1.ulcc.ac.uk
Publishes journals, *Studies in Higher Education* and *Research into Higher Education Abstracts* and books in higher education and also provides workshops and courses on a wide range of topics.

Standing Conference of National and University Libraries (SCONUL)
102 Euston Street, London, NW1 2HA
Tel: 0171 387 0317; www site: http://www.ex.ac.uk/SCONUL/
Founded in 1950, current membership includes all the universities in Ireland and the UK, together with all four national libraries: the British Library, the National Library of Ireland, the National Library of Scotland and the National Library of Wales. In conjunction with UCISA it has designed an *aide-mémoire* for assessors relating to library and IT issues.

Teaching and Learning Technology Programme (TLTP)
TLTP Co-ordinator, Northavon House, Coldharbour Lane, Bristol, BS16 1QD
Tel: 0117 931 7216; www site: http://www. tltp.ac.uk/
Set up by the UFC in 1992 inviting bids for funding for projects to develop new methods of teaching and learning through the use of technology. TLTP organizes workshops, publishes a regular newsletter and provides an update on the courseware materials available.

University and Colleges Admissions Service (UCAS)
Fulton House, Jessop Avenue, Cheltenham, Gloucestershire, GL50 3SH
Tel: 01242 227 788; www site: http://www.ucas.ac.uk/
Provides a central admissions service for applicants to courses in further education and higher education institutions in the UK.

Universities and Colleges Information Systems Association (UCISA)
UCISA Administration, University of Central England, Perry Barr, Birmingham, B42 2SU
Tel: 0121 331 6234; www site: http://www.ucisa.ac.uk/
Represents the higher education community in the provision and development of academic, management and administrative information systems. In conjunction with SCONUL, UCISA designed an *aide-mémoire* for assessors relating to IT and library issues.

Universities' and Colleges' Staff Development Agency (UCoSDA)
The University of Sheffield, Ingram House, 65 Wilkinson Street, Sheffield, S10 2GJ
Tel: 0114 222 4211; www site: http://www.niss.ac.uk/education/ucosda.html
An agency of the CVCP, set up in 1989, UCoSDA conducts research and promotes continuing professional development among academics. At present it provides the bulk of the training for assessors. It offer a full range of developmental services and consultancy to member institutions, and issues regular resource packs containing books, reports, briefing papers, etc. Non-members and individuals may purchase such materials directly from the address above.

Bibliography

Alderman, G (1996) 'Quality assessment in England: a worm in the bud?', in *Proceedings of The Eighth International Conference on Assessing Quality in Higher Education, July 14–16, 1996*, T W Banja and J L Lambert (eds), Indiana University, Indiana.

Baume, C and Baume, D (1992) *Course Design for Active Learning: Effective learning and teaching in higher education, module 2*, CVCP/USDU, Sheffield.

Brown, G and Atkins, M (1988) *Effective Teaching in Higher Education*, Routledge, London.

Brown, S, Jones, G and Rawnsley, S (1993) *Observing Teaching*, SEDA Paper 79, Staff and Educational Development Association, Birmingham.

Burge, S, Jackson, N and Tannock, J (1996) *Specification for a Quality Management Framework at Departmental Level*, Occasional Papers No. 9, Engineering Professors' Council, c/o Department of Civil and Environmental Engineering, University College London.

Campbell, G (1995) *TQA: The Chair's Report to the Association*, English Association, Leicester.

CHES (Centre for Higher Education Studies) (1994) *Assessment of the Quality of Higher Education: A review and evaluation*, CHES, London.

Cotton, J (1995a) *The Theory of Assessment: An introduction*, Kogan Page, London.

Cotton, J (1995b) *The Theory of Learning: An introduction*, Kogan Page, London.

Cotton, J (1995c) *The Theory of Learning Strategies: An introduction*, Kogan Page, London.

Cox, B (1994) *Practical Pointers for University Teachers*, Kogan Page, London.

Cox, B and Ingleby, A (1997) 'A procedure for designing an evaluation and development strategy for educational provision to suit local needs', in *Evaluating the Student Experience; Proceedings of the BI-AIR Ninth Annual*

Forum, Further Education Development Agency (FEDA), Blagdon.

DfEE (1996) News 158/96 *Membership and Terms of Reference of the National Committee of Inquiry into Higher Education Announced*, Department for Education and Employment, London.

Dixon, S (1995) *Quality Assurance in Colleges*, FEDA, London.

Ellington, H, Percival, F and Race, P (1993) *Handbook of Educational Technology*, Kogan Page, London.

Entwistle, N, Thompson, S and Tait, H (1992) *Guidelines for Providing Effective Teaching in Higher Education*, Centre for Research on Learning and Instruction, University of Edinburgh, Edinburgh.

Falchikov, N (1995) 'Improving feedback to and from students', in *Assessment for Learning in Higher Education*, P Knight (ed.), Kogan Page, London.

FEDA (Further Education Development Agency) (1995) *The Preparation of Self-Assessment Reports*, FEDA, London.

FEFC (Further Education Funding Council) (1993) *Assessing Achievement*, Circular 93/28, FEFC, Coventry.

FEFC (1994a) *Guide for Governors*, FEFC, Coventry.

FEFC (1994b) *Measuring Achievement*, Circular 94/31, FEFC, Coventry.

FEFC (1994c) *College Strategic Plans*, Circular 94/01, FEFC, Coventry.

FEFC (1997) *Validating Self-assessment*, Circular 97/12, FEFC, Coventry.

Follett, B (Chairman) (1993) *Joint Funding Council's Libraries Review Group Report*, Higher Education Funding Council for England, Bristol.

FEU (Further Education Unit) (1989) *Towards an Educational Audit*, FEU, London.

FEU (1995) 'Making Quality your Own', A discussion paper, FEU, London.

Gibbs, G (1989) *Creating a Teaching Profile*, Technical and Educational Services, Bristol.

Gibbs, G (1992) *Improving the Quality of Student Learning*, Technical and Educational Services, Bristol.

Gibbs, G, Habeshaw, S and Habeshaw, T (1989) *53 Interesting Ways to Appraise Your Teaching*, 2nd edn, Technical and Educational Services, Bristol.

Gibbs, G, Rust, C, Jenkins, A and Jaques, D (1994) *Developing Students' Transferable Skills*, The Oxford Centre for Staff Development, Oxford Bookes University.

Gordon, G and Partington, P (1993) *Quality in Higher Education: Overview and update*, UCoSDA Briefing Paper 3, UCoSDA, University of Sheffield.

Gordon, G and Partington, P (1995) *Quality in Higher Education: 1995 Update*, UCoSDA Briefing Paper 18, UCoSDA, University of Sheffield.

Gow, L and Kember, D (1993) 'Conceptions of teaching and their relationship to student learning', *British Journal of Educational Psychology*, **63**, 20–33.

Gronlund, N E (1978) 2nd edn, *Stating Objectives for Classroom Instruction*, Macmillan, New York.

HEFCE (Higher Education Funding Council for England) (1993) Circular 3/93 *Assessment of the Quality of Education*, HEFCE, Bristol.

HEFCE (1994a) Consultation Paper CP 2/94 *Further Development of the Method of the Assessment of the Quality of Education* (June 1994), HEFCE, Bristol.

HEFCE (1994b) Circular 33/94 *Quality Assessment between April 1995 and September 1996*, HEFCE, Bristol.

HEFCE (1994c) Circular 39/94 *The Quality Assessment Method from April 1995*, HEFCE, Bristol.

HEFCE (1995a) Circular 20/95 *The Forward Programme for Quality Assessment*, HEFCE, Bristol.

HEFCE (1995b) Circular 26/95 *Quality Assessment between October 1996 and September 1998*, HEFCE, Bristol.

HEFCE (1995c) Circular 29/95 *Fund for the Development of Teaching and Learning*, HEFCE, Bristol.

HEFCE (1995d) *Quality Assessment Report Q215/95*, May 1995, Loughborough University of Technology, Chemical Engineering, HEFCE, Bristol.

HEFCE (1995e) *Report on Quality Assessment*, November 1995, HEFCE, Bristol.

HEFCE (1995f) *Evaluation of the Funding Method for Teaching*, Consultation Paper 2/95, HEFCE, Bristol.

HEFCE (1995g) Subject Overview Report QO12/95 *Quality Assessment of English 1994–95*, HEFCE, Bristol.

HEFCE (1996a) *Assessors' Handbook October 1996 to September 1998*, HEFCE, Bristol.

HEFCE (1996b) Circular 11/96 *Arrangements for Quality Assessment Visits between October 1997 and June 1998*; August 1996, HEFCE, Bristol.

HEFCE (1996c) Subject Overview Report QO3/96 *Quality Assessment of German and Related Languages 1995–96*, HEFCE, Bristol.

HEFCE (1996d) Quality Assessment Report QO190/96 *Oxford Brookes University: French January 1996*, HEFCE, Bristol.

HEFCE (1996e) Subject Overview Report QO1/96 *Quality Assessment of Chemical Engineering 1995–96*, HEFCE, Bristol.

HEFCE (1996f) Subject Overview Report QO8/96 *Quality Assessment of Sociology 1995–96*, HEFCE, Bristol.

HEFCE (1997a) Circular 3/97 *Subject/Programme Review in England and Northern Ireland between October 1998 and September 2000*, HEFCE, Bristol.

HEFCE (1997b) *Report on Quality Assessment 1995–96* (January 1997), HEFCE, Bristol.

HEFCW (Higher Education Funding Council for Wales) (1994a) *Quality Assessment in the HE Sector in Wales: 1994–95 A guide for institutions and assessors*, HEFCW, Cardiff.

HEFCW (1994b) *Partnership in Assessment: Report on the consultation with HEFCW funded institutions*, HEFCW, Cardiff.

HEFCW (1995a) *Quality Assessment Programme 1995/96: Guidelines for Assessment*, HEFCW, Cardiff.

HEFCW (1995b) *The Development of Quality Assurance in Wales: Observations of* the Higher Education Funding Council for Wales to the Secretary of State for Wales*, HEFCW, Cardiff.

HEFCW (1996) *Quality Assessment Programme 1996/97: Guidelines for Assessment*, HEFCW, Cardiff.

HEQC (Higher Education Quality Council) (1994a) *Guidelines on Quality Assurance*, HEQC, London.

HEQC (1994b) *Learning from Audit 1*, HEQC, London.

HEQC (1996a) *Graduate Standards Programme*, HEQC, London.

HEQC (1996b) *Learning from Audit 2*, HEQC, London.

HEQC (1996c) *Inter-institutional variability of degree results*, HEQC, London.

HEQC (1997) *Annual Review 1995–96*, HEQC, London.

Higgins, C, Reading, J and Taylor, P (1996) *Researching into Learning Resources in Colleges and Universities*, Kogan Page, London.

Jenkins, A and Walker, L (1994) *Developing Student Capability Through Modular Courses*, Kogan Page, London.

Jones, M, Siraj-Blatchford, J and Ashcroft, K (1997) *Researching into Student Learning and Support in Colleges and Universities*, Kogan Page, London.

JPG (Joint Planning Group) (1996) *Joint Planning Group for Quality Assurance in Higher Education, Final Report* (December 1996), HEFCE, Bristol.

Kenworthy, N and Hunt, B (1993) *The Churchill Livingstone Professional Portfolio, Nurses, Midwives and Health Visitors*, Churchill Livingstone, London.

Lago, C and Shipton, G (1995) *Personal Tutoring in Action: A Handbook for Staff Who Work with and Support Students*, University of Sheffield, Sheffield.

Laurillard, D (1993) *Rethinking University Teaching: A framework for the effective use of educational technology*, Routledge, London.

Laycock, M (1996) *Quality Improvement in Learning and Teaching (QILT): A whole institutional approach to quality enhancement*, UCoSDA Briefing Paper 32, UCoSDA, Sheffield.

Mager, R F (1990) *Preparing Instructional Objectives*, 2nd edn, Kogan Page, London.

Marks, E (1996) *The Times Higher Education Supplement*, 27 September.

Marsh, H W (1987) 'Students' evaluations of university teaching: Research findings, methodological issues and directions for future research', *International Journal of Educational Research*, **2**, 3, 294.

Newton, J (1996) *Teaching Quality Assessment: Distinctive features of the methodology of the Higher Education Funding Council for Wales (HEFCW)*, UCoSDA Briefing Paper 39, UCoSDA, Sheffield.

NUS (1997) *Course Reps Resource Pack*, NUS, London.

O'Neil, M J and Pennington, G (1992) *Evaluating Teaching and Courses from an Active Learning Perspective*, CVCP/USDU, Sheffield.

Open University (1990) *Learning Strategies in Continuing Education and Training: Approaches, methods and aids*, Learning Strategies in Continuing Education and Training Project Team, Open University, Milton Keynes.

Partington, P (ed.) (1993) *Student Feedback: Context, issues and practice*,

CVCP/USDU, Sheffield.

Partington, J, Brown, G and Gordon, G (1993) *Handbook for External Examiners in Higher Education*, TLTP Project Alter in collaboration with the UK Universities' Staff Development Unit and the Universities of Kent and Leeds and Sheffield.

QCS (Quality Support Centre) (1995) *The External Examiner System: Possible Futures*, Report of a project commissioned by the HEQC, H Silver, A Stenett and R Williams, QSC, London.

QSC (1996) *Quality Assessment and Improvement: An analysis of the Recommendations made by Assessors*, T Brennan, T Shah and R Williams, QSC, London.

Ramsden, P and Dodds, A (1989) *Improving Teaching and Courses: A guide to evaluation*, 2nd edn, Centre for the Study of Higher Education, The University of Melbourne, Victoria.

Redman, W (1994) *Portfolios for Development*, Kogan Page, London.

Romiszowski, A J (1988) *The Selection and Use of Instructional Media: For improved classroom teaching and for interactive, individualised instruction*, 2nd edn, Kogan Page, London.

Rowntree, D (1981) *Developing Courses for Students*, McGraw Hill, Maidenhead.

Rowntree, D (1982) *Educational Technology in Curriculum Development*, 2nd edn, Harper & Row, London.

Rowntree, D (1987) *Assessing Students: How shall we know them?* Kogan Page, London.

Seldin, P (1997) *The Teaching Portfolio: A practical guide to improved performance and promotion/tenure decisions*, 2nd edn, Anker Publishing, Bolton, MA.

SHEFC (Scottish Higher Education Funding Council) (1996) *Quality Assessment Annual Report 1994–95*, SHEFC, Edinburgh.

SHEFC (1997) *Quality Assessment 1997–98*, SHEFC, Edinburgh.

SHEFC-COSHEP (1996) *Report of the SHEFC-COSHEP Joint Review Group on Quality Assessment*, SHEFC, Edinburgh.

UCML (University Council of Modern Languages) (1996) *Assessing the Assessors. A report by the University Council of Modern Languages on the 1995/1996 Quality Assessment Exercise in Languages*, H Footitt, UCML, London.

UCoSDA and Loughborough University (1996) *Making the Grade: Achieving high quality assessment profiles*, UCoSDA, Sheffield.

Index